Achieving your PTLLS Award

A Practical Guide to
Successful Teaching in the
Lifelong Learning Sector

2nd Edition

Mary Francis
Jim Gould

Los Angeles | London | New Delhi
Singapore | Washington DC

Los Angeles | London | New Delhi
Singapore | Washington DC

SAGE Publications Ltd
1 Oliver's Yard
55 City Road
London EC1Y 1SP

SAGE Publications Inc.
2455 Teller Road
Thousand Oaks, California 91320

SAGE Publications India Pvt Ltd
B 1/I 1 Mohan Cooperative Industrial Area
Mathura Road
New Delhi 110 044

SAGE Publications Asia-Pacific Pte Ltd
3 Church Street
#10-04 Samsung Hub
Singapore 049483

Editor: Marianne Lagrange
Editorial assistant: Kathryn Bromwich
Production editor: Thea Watson
Copyeditor: Rosemary Campbell
Proofreader: Derek Markham
Marketing manager: Catherine Slinn
Cover design: Wendy Scott
Typeset by: C&M Digitals (P) Ltd, Chennai, India
Printed by: MPG Books Group, Bodmin, Cornwall

Library of Congress Control Number: 2012933799

British Library Cataloguing in Publication data

A catalogue record for this book is available from the British Library

ISBN 978-1-4462-4979-6
ISBN 978-1-4462-4980-2 (pbk)

Contents

Acknowledgements viii
Introduction ix
   Features of the book ix
   The symbols you will meet and what they mean xi

**1 Working in the lifelong learning sector – roles,
   responsibilities and boundaries** 1
   Working in the lifelong learning sector 1
   Ensuring a professional workforce 3
   Roles, responsibilities and relationships of teachers
      in the lifelong learning sector 3
   Legislative requirements 7
   Establishing professional and personal boundaries 8
   Making use of internal and external support 10

2 Establishing a positive learning environment 12
   Aspects of the environment 12
   The physical environment and patterns of communication .. 13
   The social environment – first impressions,
      ground rules, breaking the ice 15
   A positive approach to teaching 22

3 Communicating with learners 24
   Defining communication 24
   Effective communication – a model 25
   Non-verbal communication 29
   Barriers to communication 31

4 Motivating learners and managing behaviour 34
   Motivation 34
   Approaches to behaviour management 38
   Self concept 40
   Responses to inappropriate behaviour 41

5 Starting to plan 48
   What to consider in planning 49
   The sequence in planning 50
   Aims and objectives 53
   Choosing appropriate methods 59

6	**Planning for inclusive learning**	**63**
	Initial assessment of learners	64
	Individual differences	65
	Diversity	67
	Inclusion	68
	Differentiation	68
	Equality	71
7	**Learning individually and in groups**	**75**
	Working with groups	75
	What is a group?	75
	Moving towards a performing group	77
	Different forms of group work	78
	Managing group work	79
	Working one-to-one	83
8	**Teaching your specialism**	**88**
	Theory-based subjects	89
	Question and answer	93
	Skill-based subjects	96
	Attitudinally-based subjects	102
9	**Effective use of resources**	**111**
	How resources support learning	111
	The range of resources	112
	Designing resources for impact and purpose	114
	Making effective use of resources	116
	E-resources	120
	Evaluating resources	125
10	**Assessing learning**	**128**
	Assessment methods	129
	Purposes of assessment	132
	Selecting appropriate methods	134
	Validity and reliability	136
	When do we assess?	139
	Who assesses?	140
	Designing assessments	141
	Preparing learners to succeed in assessment	141
	Constructive feedback	143
	Record keeping	144
11	**Competence-based assessment**	**147**
	Assessing competence	147
	Structure of vocational qualifications	148
	Roles in vocational assessment	149
	Stages in competence-based assessment	149
	Improving your assessor skills	153
	Checklist for competence-based assessment	153

12 **Supporting Functional Skills development**   **155**
   What are Functional Skills?   155
   Mapping and embedding Functional Skills   159
   Benefits of embedding Functional Skills   160

13 **Developing session plans**   **167**
   The purpose of planning   167
   Planning decisions   169
   Structuring a session plan   172

14 **Evaluating learning**   **183**
   Why evaluate?   183
   How to evaluate   185
   Action planning   192

15 **Microteaching**   **196**
   Microteaching explained   196
   Planning for microteaching   197
   Being positive about microteaching   202
   Delivering the session   204
   After the microteaching session   204
   Where next?   206

Appendices   **208**
   Appendix 1 Mapping the content of the book
      against PTLLS requirements   208
   Appendix 2 Example session plans   210
   Appendix 3 Citing and referencing   215

Glossary of terms   219
Index   222

Acknowledgements

The authors are grateful to the following for their contributions and suggestions: Caroline Allen, Dave Baber, Suzanne Dunsmore, Sara Halsey, Pip Kings, Kieran Allen Lowe, Pauline Mason, Stephen Norris, Yvette Raikes, Julie Ralphs, Esther Schmitz and Alan Woods.

Drawings are by Lisa Bailey.

The quote by Geoff Petty on page 216 is reproduced with the permission of Nelson Thornes Ltd from *Teaching Today: A Practical Guide* (Fourth Edition), Geoff Petty, 978-1-4085-0415-4, first published in 2009.

Introduction

We work in a fast-changing sector. This second edition of *Achieving your PTLLS Award* provides a timely opportunity to update what has proved a popular book and to align its content with the latest requirements for the Levels 3 and 4 Awards 'Preparing to Teach in the Lifelong Learning Sector'.

The PTLLS Awards are now worth 12 credit points at each level and contain four units:

- Roles, responsibilities and relationships in lifelong learning
- Understanding inclusive learning and teaching in lifelong learning
- Using inclusive learning and teaching in lifelong learning
- Principles of assessment in lifelong learning.

To help you achieve these new units, we have used this opportunity to develop a new chapter related to learning individually and in groups and added a Chapter on competence-based assessment. As well as appealing to those who will teach or train in the lifelong learning sector, this book will also appeal to those who may be working in training functions in both the private and public sectors, and to those who may be working towards a Learning and Development (L&D) qualification or taking stand-alone L&D units. For example:

- Facilitating learning and development with individuals/in groups (Level 3)
- Manage learning and development in groups (Level 4)
- Understanding the principles and practices of assessment (Levels 3 and 4).

Features of the book

Each chapter of this book has the following features:

- An overview and rationale so that you have a complete picture of chapter content and understand its intended outcomes, structure and importance
- A mix of short exercises and reflective questions to encourage you to reflect upon the issues. This will be either from the perspective of your own experience, if you are currently in a teaching or training role, or as areas for consideration if you are a prospective rather than a practising teacher or trainer
- Prompts for you to record your reflections
- Discussion of appropriate/expected responses, to provide you with feedback
- At the end of each chapter, a summary of the main learning points covered
- Suggested websites and further reading, annotated to give you a brief overview of the nature and level of the book and the relevant areas to consult.

Here are some questions you will want answered as you begin to use this book.

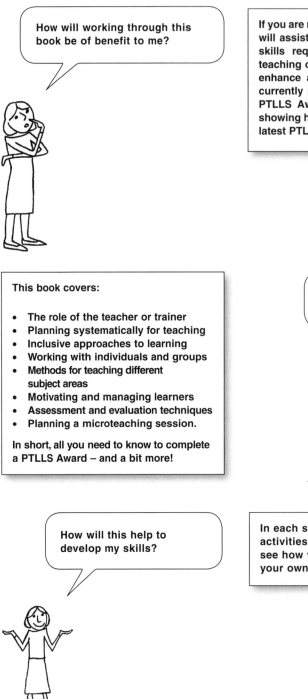

How will working through this book be of benefit to me?

If you are new to teaching or training this book will assist you to acquire the knowledge and skills required. If you already have some teaching or training experience, it will help to enhance and further develop the skills you currently possess. To help you achieve your PTLLS Award, there is a map (Appendix 1) showing how the content matches each of the latest PTLLS requirements.

This book covers:

- The role of the teacher or trainer
- Planning systematically for teaching
- Inclusive approaches to learning
- Working with individuals and groups
- Methods for teaching different subject areas
- Motivating and managing learners
- Assessment and evaluation techniques
- Planning a microteaching session.

In short, all you need to know to complete a PTLLS Award – and a bit more!

What sort of information is contained in the book?

How will this help to develop my skills?

In each section you will find a number of activities. By completing these, you will see how you can apply the information to your own particular situation.

The symbols you will meet and what they mean

Chapter overview

Outlines what you will work through in this chapter. The bullet points in the box show what you will achieve after completing the chapter.

Activity box

Read and apply what you have read to your own teaching or learning situation.

Chapter summary

When you reach the chapter summary box, this is an opportunity for you to make sure you have taken in all the main points made so far before going on to the next chapter.

Further reading

Photocopiable

This page can be photocopied.

Useful websites

Suggested books and websites related to the content of the particular chapter which will enable you to further develop your thinking.

At the end of the book you will find:

- Appendices, including example session plans
- A glossary explaining the main terms used in the text.

You can find helpful photocopiable session plans, activities and checklists at www.sagepub.co.uk/francisandgould

1

Working in the lifelong learning sector – roles, responsibilities and boundaries

Chapter overview

When you have completed this chapter on working in the lifelong learning sector you will be able to:

- Describe what is meant by the 'lifelong learning sector'
- Explain the drive towards professionalism in the lifelong learning sector and its implications for those working in it
- Review the roles, responsibilities and boundaries of professionals in the sector
- Identify points of referral to meet the potential needs of learners
- Recognise key aspects of relevant current legislative requirements and codes of practice relevant to your own context

Working in the lifelong learning sector

If you are reading this book we expect that you are currently working or preparing to teach or train in the lifelong learning sector and may well be interested in gaining the PTLLS Award.

What does the lifelong learning sector look like? It is a sector that covers all publicly funded post-16 education, excluding universities; this takes place in a wide range of institutions, including Further Education (FE) colleges, adult and community education, private training providers of work-based learning, libraries, archives and information services, voluntary sector organisations and prisons. Some interesting facts about the lifelong learning sector emerge:

1 Over two-thirds of learners are 19+ and part time.
2 There are more 16–19 year olds in colleges of FE than in sixth forms in secondary schools.
3 Learners range from those who cannot read, write or communicate, to those at post-degree level.
4 There are more students in FE colleges than in universities.
5 One in five adults are currently learning, with over one-third of adults having participated in some learning activity during the last three years.
6 Approximately £15 billion was spent on this sector in 2010–11, £11 billion of this on young people.
7 The majority of the workforce is female.
8 Part-time teaching staff in FE outnumber full-time teaching staff by almost 2:1.

Is this a picture that you recognise? The roles of professionals in the lifelong learning sector are extremely diverse; you may be called a lecturer, a tutor, a trainer, an instructor, an assessor, a work-based learning or an apprentice supervisor, or a learning manager. Some of you may have gained skills and experience through another trade or profession, for example as an engineer, hairdresser, nurse or bricklayer. Whilst some of you may also be teaching 14–16 year olds in FE, what you are likely to have in common is that you will all have a teaching or training function with learners aged 16 and above. Some of you may have broader training functions, for example in the Fire, Police or Armed Services, or be training staff in-house within a public or private organisation. For the purpose of this book we will use the term 'teacher' generically to apply to all these various roles and 'learner' to apply to those who you may also call students, pupils, employees, trainees or apprentices.

Professional teachers in the lifelong learning sector also share in the common purpose of serving the needs of learners, employers and the community. They face the challenges of working in a context which is diverse and rapidly changing.

The last decade has seen significant political and economic change impacting on the sector. For instance, in the area of funding, in April 2010, responsibilities for those aged 16–19 and 19+ were separated. The Young People's Learning Agency (YPLA) and Skills Funding Agency were set up to take over from the Learning and Skills Council (itself only established in 2001); and local authorities took on enhanced responsibilities for planning and funding 14–19 year olds' education and training.

The YPLA was closed in March 2012 and a new executive agency of the Department for Education, the Education Funding Agency (EFA) was established. The EFA has responsibility for calculating funding for all 16–19 education and training, in accordance with a national funding policy, including 16–19 provision in Further Education colleges and up to 25 for learners with learning difficulties and disabilities (LLDD). It directly funds the growing number of academies and Free Schools, sixth form colleges, and independent provision. The local authorities act as strategic commissioners of provision for young people aged 16–19 (16–25 for LLDD); funding for school sixth forms is routed from the EFA via local authorities.

The Skills Funding Agency, a partner organisation of the Department for Business, Innovation and Skills (BIS), is responsible for funding and regulating Further Education and adult skills with the aim of enabling people to do their jobs better, get new jobs, or progress in their careers. It houses the National Apprenticeship Service.

It is evident then that the lifelong learning sector has been in a state of frequent change, as government strives to raise the overall level of skills and ensure the UK is competitive in the world economy. As lifelong learning professionals you are expected to play a key role in helping more young people and adults participate in education and training and succeed in achieving appropriate qualifications.

Ensuring a professional workforce

Teacher qualifications for the Learning and Skills sector have also undergone significant change over the last five years. All teachers, trainers and tutors offered jobs in colleges and other publicly funded organisations are expected to have an appropriate teaching qualification. The Lingfield Report (BIS, 2012a), however, recommends deregulating FE teaching qualifications. Following consultation, the government will take a staged approach to deregulation; removing 'elements that are dependent on mandatory IfL [Institute for Learning] registration… [whilst] the core requirements for minimum qualifications will be retained for the 2012/13 academic year' (BIS, 2012b: 8). It proposes to set up an FE Guild to support self-regulation and for the Learning and Skills Improvement Service (LSIS) to undertake a review of the current qualification structure.

If you are preparing to teach in the lifelong learning sector it is likely that you will still be expected to undergo an appropriate induction and foundation in teaching such as the Award in Preparing to Teach in the Lifelong Learning Sector (PTLLS), the current 'threshold license to teach'. This book focuses on helping you to achieve the PTLLS Award or a similar foundation level qualification.

Roles, responsibilities and relationships of teachers in the lifelong learning sector

In this section we will begin to consider your work in the lifelong learning sector; as we have seen above it is a much more diverse sector than the schools sector. We will focus on the following two questions:

1   What roles are you expected to fulfil?
2   What are the specific responsibilities and boundaries associated with these roles?

When we talk about a 'role' most people instantly think of playing a part, or acting in some capacity. A role involves some idea of expected behaviour associated with a position. You will have expectations of the learners or students that you will teach, train, assess or tutor. These may include an expectation that they will study and undergo assessments.

When we look at the role of a teacher, trainer, assessor or tutor we find that there is a body of agreed expectations associated with these roles.

Activity 1.1

What do you expect someone who is a lecturer, teacher, trainer, assessor or tutor in the lifelong learning sector to do?

Now look at these three examples of a typical day of a lifelong learning professional:

Case study 1 – Assessor in the workplace

Travel to employer premises

Review a portfolio

Meet a candidate and check underpinning knowledge

Discuss learner progress with another assessor

Attend an internal verification meeting

Lunch

Identify Functional Skills needs of a candidate

Candidate is having problems gaining experience to demonstrate their competence. Talk to workplace supervisor

Conduct a tutorial on Skype

Fill out travel expenses claim form

Check the latest Sector Skills Council update

Case study 2 – FE lecturer

Arrive at college, check pigeon hole

Check preparation for first lesson, last minute photocopying

Give first part of lesson

Break – check college emails

Give second part of lesson

Lesson finished – deal with related administration

Give new part-time colleague advice on initial assessment

Get lunch from canteen

Discuss discipline problem with a colleague

Answer two telephone calls relating to course enquiries

Eat (now cold) lunch

Help a tutee with personal statement and UCAS form

Accept sick note from tutee, and mark register/tutorial notes

Scan internal memos

Prepare mark sheet for exam

Teach lesson

Update virtual learning environment (VLE) and check assignment drop-boxes

Mark assignments ready for tutorial

Review learner minimum grade expectations on college intranet

Give tutorial

Share resources with colleague

Case study 3 – Voluntary sector worker

Organise a room for a briefing session with volunteer tutors

Plan an introductory session

Take the register

Conduct an ice breaker

Explain the volunteer role

Discuss volunteer placements and process for Criminal Record Bureau (CRB) checks

Complete learner records

Telephone a volunteer who missed the session

Meet a volunteer who is having problems relating to an autistic learner

Fill out an application for funding for a future course

Check charity website for publicity on Volunteer Training programme

Activity 1.2

What do these three roles have in common?

The first thing that will probably strike you is that a lot of time is spent in activities that are not directly concerned with imparting knowledge or skills. You will probably come to the conclusion that the role of a teacher has many sub-roles, and so equally do other roles in the lifelong learning sector.

These may include any or all of the following:

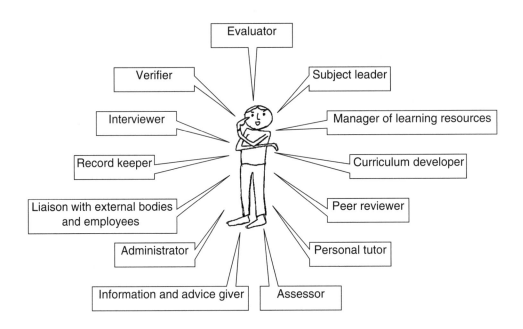

Activity 1.3

Thinking of your own context, what role do you expect to play? Looking at the diagram above note any sub-roles you have. Are there any that have been overlooked that you need to add?

Which of these do you consider to be your core 'professional' roles?

With each of these sub-roles come associated responsibilities; these will be shaped by national legislation (for example, Health and Safety), institutional requirements (for example, the responsibility to ensure a policy on lateness or Internet access is consistently carried out) and situational requirements (for example, responsibility to ensure no eating or drinking in a computer room). These associated responsibilities imply dependability, conscientiousness and trustworthiness on the part of the teacher.

A key responsibility of a teacher in the lifelong learning sector, for example, is the checking and reporting of learner attendance and achievement. This is necessary for monitoring progress of learners and in order for the organisation to report accurately to governors, funding and inspection bodies. Largely, however, the responsibilities of a lifelong learning professional involve 'doing a proper job' by, for example:

- Treating all learners fairly and with equal respect (Equality and Diversity)
- Giving learners the opportunity to participate on equal terms and with an equal expectation of success (Equality)
- Engaging and involving all learners in relevant activities (Inclusion)
- Keeping learners safe (Safeguarding)
- Acknowledging and celebrating the diversity in a group of learners (Differentiation)
- Planning to meet the needs and styles of individual learners (Personalisation)
- Keeping up to date with subject developments
- Being well prepared
- Returning marked work in a reasonable time.

Legislative requirements

The lifelong learning professional also has a responsibility to ensure that current legislative requirements are met. Whilst some legislation and codes of practice are at least in part subject related, there is a considerable body of legislation that applies to the lifelong learning sector as a whole. Legislation and associated policy are constantly changing, however, as evidenced by the Education and Skills Act 2008; the Apprenticeships, Skills, Children and Learning Act 2009; and the Education Act 2011; and it is important to keep up to date with the current position as it affects us (see www.legislation.gov.uk).

The 'Every Child Matters: Change for Children' (ECM) and the related provisions in the Children Act 2004 provide an example of this. ECM promotes the well-being of children and young people aged 0–19 and vulnerable adults through five outcomes: Be healthy; Stay safe; Enjoy and achieve; Make a positive contribution; and Achieve economic well-being. Following recent legislation there is still a duty to co-operate to improve outcomes for children as defined by the ECM outcomes, however, how this is achieved is now less prescriptive.

Allied to this is the Protection of Children Act (1999), whereby teachers who come into contact with children or vulnerable adults are subject to the 'enhanced check' by the Criminal Records Bureau (CRB), and the subsequent Safeguarding Vulnerable Groups Act (2006). When FE colleges are inspected, inspectors evaluate the extent to which learners are safeguarded and protected, and ask the question 'How safe do learners feel?' (Ofsted, 2012: 48).

Inspectors will be looking for evidence relating to:

- The extent to which learners feel that the learning environment is safe and welcoming, and that all individuals are respected equally
- The extent to which staff take action to identify and respond appropriately to learners' welfare concerns
- Learners' understanding and use of Internet safety measures

and these will be your concerns as well.

These are merely two examples of legislation which affect you. The list below provides other examples:

1 Legislation relating to Health and Safety – the responsibility to provide a safe environment, both physical and psychological:

   - Health & Safety at Work Act (1974)
   - Manual Handling Operations Regulations (1992)
   - RIDDOR – Reporting of Injuries, Diseases and Dangerous Occurrences Regulations (1995)
   - Management of the Health & Safety at Work Act (1999)
   - COSHH – Control of Substances Hazardous to Health Regulations (2002)

A useful website for keeping up to date with current Health and Safety requirements is www.hse.gov.uk

2 Legislation relating to Human Rights – a new Equality Act (2010) harmonised and streamlined existing legislation such as the Disability and Discrimination Act 1995, Sex Discrimination Act 1975 and Race Relations Act 1976. It also extended equality provision to cover the following nine 'protected characteristics': age, disability, race, religion or belief, sex, sexual orientation, gender reassignment, married and civil partnerships, and pregnant or having just had a baby. From April 2011 public sector bodies have a duty to have due regard to eliminate discrimination, advance equality of opportunity and foster good relations between people from different groups.

In more general terms, legislation such as The Copyright Design and Patents Act (1988) and The Data Protection Act (1998) also impact on working life and habits within the sector. In your role in lifelong learning you will therefore need to adhere to the legislation outlined above and have particular awareness of any legislative responsibilities relevant to the teaching of your subject.

Establishing professional and personal boundaries

If we perform the roles required of us, with their associated responsibilities, we exemplify 'professionalism' in the work we do. Professionalism requires us to maintain appropriate standards and fulfil our responsibilities to learners, institutions and colleagues.

Teachers in the lifelong learning sector work with a range of other professionals and support staff. The way in which we perform our role can be influenced by these others: for example learners or line managers, each with their own particular roles to fulfil. This group with whom you relate in your role as a teacher can have significant impact on how you act as a teacher.

Activity 1.4

Think about your own professional context. Identify all the people with whom you come into contact, each of whom has their own particular role to play.

These various roles, taken together, form your 'role set', particular to your own situation. It may include managers, support staff (librarians, technicians, reprographic staff), administrators, finance, counsellors, union representatives, employers and governors. Those who make up your role set can often place conflicting demands on you as a teacher, pulling you in different directions; this is known as role strain.

Activity 1.5

If you look at your role set above, what two roles might expect you to act in two different ways? What kind of role strain might develop?

Some tutors in adult and community education find a considerable strain results from the caretaker imposing demands about room layout and getting students out of the class promptly at the end of the evening. This may make it difficult for you to meet expectations from your line manager that you will resolve an issue with an individual learner when you still need five minutes to find a way forward.

Because individuals with whom you work may place what you consider to be unacceptable demands on you, it is necessary to have a clear idea as to how you see your role and what you should do in order to fulfil it. Professional relationships can be aided by setting clear professional and personal boundaries; this is an important aspect of professionalism. In this context a boundary is a limit on the extent of involvement. Which of the issues in Activity 1.6 do you think fall within your professional boundaries?

Activity 1.6

If a learner presents one of the following problems, do you consider it falls within your role and responsibilities as a teacher in the lifelong learning sector? If not, to whom could you refer this issue?

- Abuse
- Bereavement
- Bullying
- Career issues
- Financial problems
- Study skills
- Illness
- Depression
- Failing
- Prolonged absence
- Relationship breakdowns
- Stress

Making use of internal and external support

In the activity above you have identified areas that you consider to be outside your professional boundaries. Either you think it is inappropriate to deal with these or feel that you do not have the necessary skills or expertise. Support from someone else will be needed, and it is important that you can identify who this might be. Institutions have a range of support systems and you should check out your organisational structure chart to see what is available internally to supplement your work with learners.

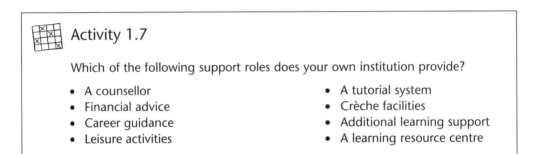

Activity 1.7

Which of the following support roles does your own institution provide?

- A counsellor
- Financial advice
- Career guidance
- Leisure activities
- A tutorial system
- Crèche facilities
- Additional learning support
- A learning resource centre

Learners can present a variety of problems which may prevent them from making progress with their studies or life plans. You will be better able to help them if you are fully aware of the internal and external support mechanisms which are available to them.

In this chapter we have focused on your role as a professional in the lifelong learning sector. In the following chapters we will explore different aspects of this role and associated responsibilities, starting with your responsibility as a teacher to create an appropriate environment in which learning can take place.

Chapter summary

The main points covered in this chapter are:

- ✓ Lifelong learning encompasses a range of different types of provision.
- ✓ The role of the teacher in the lifelong learning sector is not confined to imparting knowledge and skills but covers a multiplicity of different tasks.
- ✓ Roles are accompanied by responsibilities and these contribute to the adoption of a professional approach to work in the lifelong learning sector.
- ✓ A professional approach involves being aware of and upholding current legislation and codes of practice.
- ✓ The relationship between your role and that of others with whom you work may sometimes lead to tensions or 'role strain'.
- ✓ Teachers in the lifelong learning sector need to be aware of both professional boundaries and their own personal limitations, knowing when and to whom to refer learners for further support.

→ References

Department for Business, Innovation and Skills (BIS) (2012a) *Professionalism in Further Education: Interim Report.* London: Department for Business, Innovation and Skills.

Department for Business, Innovation and Skills (BIS) (2012b) *Consultation on Revocation of the Further Education Workforce Regulations: Government Response.* London: Department for Business, Innovation and Skills.

Ofsted (2012) *Handbook for the Inspection of Further Education and Skills.* 2009, adapted to apply to inspections from April 2012. Available online at: www.ofsted.gov.uk/resources/090105

📖 Further reading

Coles, A. (2004) *Teaching in Post-Compulsory Education: Policy Practice and Values.* London: David Fulton Publishers.

Chapter 3 of this book directly addresses the role of the post-compulsory teacher, outlining a wide variety of sub-roles with appropriate background.

Tummons, J. (2010) *Becoming a Professional Tutor in the Lifelong Learning Sector* (2nd edn). Exeter: Learning Matters.

Chapter 2 examines the purpose of the lifelong sector and how this impacts upon the professional role, with particular reference to accountability. Chapter 3 looks at the reasons behind codes of practice and how they impact upon role.

🖱 Useful websites

LSIS

http://www.lsis.org.uk/Pages/default.aspx

The role of the teacher

http://www.prospects.ac.uk/further_education_lecturer_job_description.htm

Education Funding Agency

www.education.gov.uk/b00199952/the-education-funding-agency

Skills Funding Agency

http://skillsfundingagency.bis.gov.uk/

Health and Safety Executive

http://www.hse.gov.uk

Contains an education site and a classroom checklist

Legislation

www.legislation.gov.uk

2

Establishing a positive learning environment

Chapter overview

When you have worked through this chapter on a positive learning environment you will be able to:

- Identify the three aspects of the environment and how these contribute to a safe and supportive climate for learning
- Recognise the effects of the environment on patterns of communication
- State the need for ground rules to promote appropriate behaviour and respect for others, identifying ways of setting these
- List different methods of 'breaking the ice'

Aspects of the environment

In the next few chapters we will be looking at our learners and the decisions that have to be made in planning and delivering teaching sessions. In a sense it is like a musician preparing for a concert. The music has been chosen and practised until it can be played without mistakes. Is this enough, however, to make the concert a success?

Our musician will also be thinking about the best way to set out the concert hall. Is the audience to dance, or sit and listen? This will affect issues such as whether seating is provided, whether only the stage will be lit or the whole hall. Will there in fact be a stage? If the musician wishes the audience to join in, it may be better to sit at the same level or even in the middle of the audience.

How will our musician create a relationship or rapport with the audience, will he or she talk to them and if so, how? All of these concerns are to do with creating an appropriate environment within which the performance will take place. We have to address similar issues in any form of teaching in which we engage.

One way we can define teaching is:

The teacher creates the optimum environment in which people can learn.

What do we mean when we use the term 'environment' in this context?

One interpretation suggests the teaching environment has three aspects:

1 The **physical** environment
2 The **social** environment
3 The **learning** environment.

Although we have listed these separately, in reality each has an effect on the other and each is equally important in the planning of any teaching that we undertake.

The *learning* environment is concerned with giving the session a sense of purpose and direction. In Chapter 5, we look at how we might achieve this through the way in which we systematically plan teaching sessions; here we will focus on the other two aspects of the teaching environment.

The *physical* environment is about the surroundings within which teaching takes place, whilst the *social* environment concerns how you put your learners at ease and establish rapport with them.

Activity 2.1

1 What do you think makes a good physical environment for learning?

2 What do you think makes a good social environment for learning?

The physical environment and patterns of communication

One aspect of this environment is the actual physical conditions under which teaching takes place. Is the room too hot, too stuffy? Is it too bright or too dark for the method you plan to use?

Another aspect of the physical environment is to do with the arrangement of the furniture and resources. This is affected by two related factors:

- The methods we are using
- The kind of interaction we wish to take place.

Different methods and activities will require teachers and learners to take on different roles, which in turn will require different types of interaction. Do we want learners to take a passive role where they mainly listen and perhaps take notes? Alternatively, are we looking for them to take a more active role where they contribute, join in and discuss? Do we wish attention to be focused more on learners and their performance? Answers to these questions will influence the type of communication we will wish to encourage. This, in turn, will influence the way in which we organise the physical environment in which our teaching will take place.

We can classify communication in a number of different ways, as follows:

One-way   We talk to the learners who listen and do not contribute unless specifically asked. Attention is focused on us and on the resources we are presenting. This would be appropriate in any form of teaching in which we present information in a logical sequence.

Two-way   We talk to the learners who listen, but they will also ask questions and will be encouraged to make contributions of their own, although we would normally expect them to do this through us. A more interactive approach is sought and attention needs to be focused on whoever is speaking at the time.

Several-ways   Everyone makes contributions and asks questions, addressing the group as a whole. This situation might arise when we are having a discussion with learners, who are expressing ideas and opinions. Alternatively, if learners are seeking information for themselves, they may be doing this in small groups involving several-way communication.

Room layout

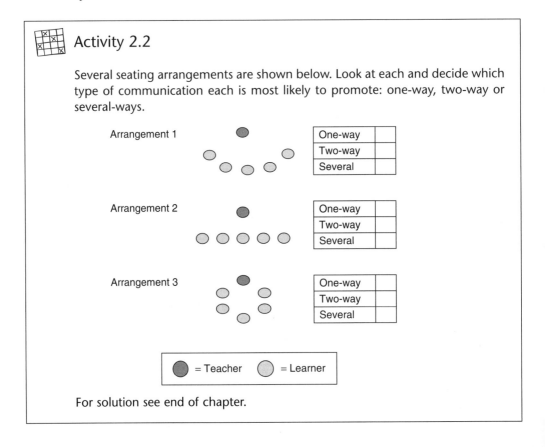

Activity 2.2

Several seating arrangements are shown below. Look at each and decide which type of communication each is most likely to promote: one-way, two-way or several-ways.

Arrangement 1

One-way	
Two-way	
Several	

Arrangement 2

One-way	
Two-way	
Several	

Arrangement 3

One-way	
Two-way	
Several	

= Teacher   = Learner

For solution see end of chapter.

Adding desks or tables also makes a difference. Consider the layout below.

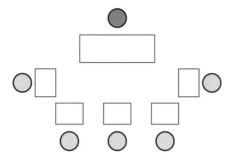

You can see that tables create a barrier; this results in a more formal learning situation. This layout tends to cut down the chances of two-way and several-ways communication. Tables also constitute a 'safety barrier', however (as well as providing a surface for writing) and learners may well feel exposed by their absence.

The way we set up the environment, whether we include tables and chairs, even whether we, as teachers, sit, stand, or move around the room, makes a difference to where attention is focused. These factors can either encourage or inhibit different patterns of communication. Workshop settings require adequate individual space to ensure safety. Some arrangements will give a 'formal' feel to the session, others a more 'informal' or relaxed feel in which the learners may feel more at ease. The key factor is the amount of eye contact that can be made.

The physical environment, however, is not the only factor that determines the atmosphere or climate within which the session takes place. To see what else plays a part we must now look to the social environment.

The social environment – first impressions, ground rules, breaking the ice

Generally, we learn best when we are relaxed and feel comfortable with what we are experiencing in the teaching environment – when we feel secure and largely free from anxiety. It is part of our role as teachers to establish such a climate for learners, but how is this achieved? There is no simple answer, as a combination of different factors is involved.

To start thinking about these, consider all of the factors that would make you feel *uncomfortable* in your learning. It may help to think back to occasions when you have been taught yourself and, in some way, found it to be an unpleasant or uncomfortable experience.

 Activity 2.3

What can make you feel uncomfortable in your learning?

Some of the factors you have considered in response to the above activity will be related to the teaching itself, and we will address these in later chapters. Some will be more to do with how you feel as a learner in the learning environment, whereas others will be to do with the teacher and their attitudes and actions. How do your thoughts compare with the lists below?

To do with how learners feel

- Lack of confidence in own ability
- Not valued or respected
- Lack of motivation
- Unsure of other learners
- Not listened to
- It's a test or a threat.

To do with the teacher's attitudes and actions

- Unenthusiastic teachers
- Disorganised or badly prepared teachers
- Teachers who are sarcastic or impatient with learners
- Teachers who foster a competitive atmosphere
- Teachers who patronise learners
- Teachers who put learners 'on the spot'
- Teachers who make premature judgements about learners
- Teachers who show little interest in their learners or do not recognise learners as individuals
- Teachers who use material which does not suit the learners.

In your own teaching sessions you will want to establish a climate very different from that indicated above. A positive social climate is unlikely to be achieved immediately, but is built up gradually. It is something that we need to work towards from the time we first meet learners.

The first meeting between the teacher and the learner or learners, is a significant time in establishing the sort of climate that is conducive to learning. One of the major aims of the first session is to reduce anxiety levels and to begin to establish some form of relationship or rapport between the teacher and learners and between the different learners themselves.

First impressions
We don't get a second chance to make a first impression, so the impression we create both individually and as an institution needs to be positive.

Institutions often have induction policies which are designed to ensure that all learners have as smooth a transition as possible into their new programmes of study and the culture and expectations of the institution.

Activity 2.4

What do you think should be included in an induction programme?

A typical induction programme will include:

- Finding your way about the site
- Introduction to staff
- Introduction to any services, such as the learning resource centre, information, advice and guidance (IAG), counselling, welfare
- Health and Safety information – procedures for fire and accidents
- Learning Agreements
- Developing your Individual Learning Plan (ILP)
- Policies, for example Complaints, Equality and Diversity.

When we first meet learners some of the things that they will notice about us are:

- Appearance – are we suitably dressed?
- Bearing – do we appear confident, open and friendly?
- Level of preparation – are we organised, structured, and well prepared?

How we 'measure up' in these areas will, at least in the first instance, determine how learners will react to us and how much confidence they will have in our ability to provide them with the sort of teaching they would want and expect.

How we dress will be a matter of personal preference, but whatever we wear, it should be appropriate to the type of teaching we will be doing. If it is a workshop environment, for instance, a white coat or overalls may be appropriate. A tracksuit is appropriate for sports coaching. In any event we should be dressed so that the learners feel we have made some effort with our appearance on their behalf.

Similarly with preparation, having the appropriate paperwork and teaching resources to hand shows we have put thought into the teaching that is to be received. This is borne out by a confident introduction and a session that flows smoothly from one section to the next.

Body language also plays its part – we should maintain good eye contact, adopt an open posture and possibly most important of all – SMILE and MEAN IT!

Openings

Our initial contact with learners can be used to dispel many of the fears and anxieties that may exist. Our manner is an important factor in this, so it helps to be welcoming and to learn and use names at the earliest opportunity (name badges or desk cards can be helpful in this respect). In any opening remarks, we are aiming to establish our credibility as teachers. This can be achieved by referring to our experience and qualifications. We do not wish to become unapproachable, so care should be taken not to overdo this. We are aiming to reassure learners of our capabilities, not scare them off.

At this stage, we would also tell them a little about the course and what they might expect from it:

- The content that will be covered
- The activities they will engage in
- Expectations of workload
- Any work related activities
- How progress will be checked
- What their part in it will be.

By doing this we are aiming to take the 'fear of the unknown' out of the teaching so that learners will feel reassured and more relaxed in their learning. A feeling of trust and confidentiality needs to be conveyed.

Ground rules

You may at this stage also wish to introduce some ground rules relating to the way you are to function together as a group. Theories of group development suggest that groups form in a series of stages. The first stage involves the coming together of the members of the potential group. This is followed by a 'jostling for position', before 'norms', or expectations of behaviour, from those in the group, begin to emerge. It is only after this last stage that the group begins to function as a working unit. We will examine group dynamics in more depth in Chapter 7.

The creating of norms, expectations or rules is a natural part of the development of a group. Learners need a sense of structure and will feel psychologically safer if they know what is expected of them. They may already have come across institutional rules relating, for instance, to zero tolerance of bullying, eating and drinking in ICT and other rooms, smoking, use of mobile phones or specific subject-related Health and Safety regulations, as part of a more general induction programme. What we are now considering is more to do with attitudes and behaviours within the immediate teaching environment.

Activity 2.5

What do you think it would be useful to include in a set of ground rules for a group that you will teach?

Exactly what you have arrived at may well depend on the nature and maturity of your learners and the setting within which you teach your particular subject.

Perhaps you may have considered:

- Punctuality, both at the beginning of sessions and returning from breaks
- Handing in work on time
- Eating, drinking and mobile phones (if not already covered by institutional rules)
- Listening when attention is asked for
- Not talking whilst others are contributing
- Respecting the rights of others to hold different points of view, whether or not you agree with them
- Not being critical of or bullying others in the group
- Keeping all that is said within the group as confidential.

Having established in your own mind what might be appropriate to include, you need to decide how to agree these rules with your learners; some may be mandatory whilst others are negotiable. Essentially there are three positions that might be adopted here, as summarised in the figure below.

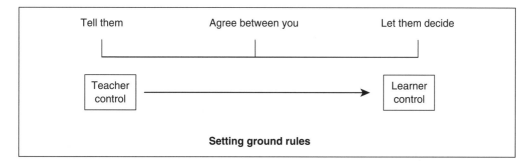

Setting ground rules

You may well use different strategies with different groups that you teach, but in arriving at a decision it is helpful to consider the following:

- The nature, size and maturity of the group may make one approach more appropriate than the others
- The confidence that you have in yourself and your ability to control or influence the group will affect the approach you choose
- The further towards the 'teacher control' end of the continuum you go, the more learners will consider the rules to be your rules, and therefore your responsibility to enforce them
- The further towards the 'learner control' end of the continuum you go, the more learners will see the rules as their rules and thus have a greater commitment to both the rules themselves and the enforcing of them.

 Activity 2.6

What do you think is the most appropriate method of setting ground rules for your own group(s)?

Breaking the ice

By this stage we will have established some rapport with our learners but we may also want learners to work and to learn together in a supportive manner. If this is the case learners need to become acquainted and comfortable with each other.

This will take time, but the process can be initiated by introducing an 'icebreaker' at the start of teaching. An icebreaker is any activity which encourages learners to talk to us, to each other and to the group as a whole. It is designed to break down the barriers that invariably exist when a group of people meets for the first time.

Icebreakers range from 'short and sharp' to 'extended' activities and can be divided into the three categories shown below.

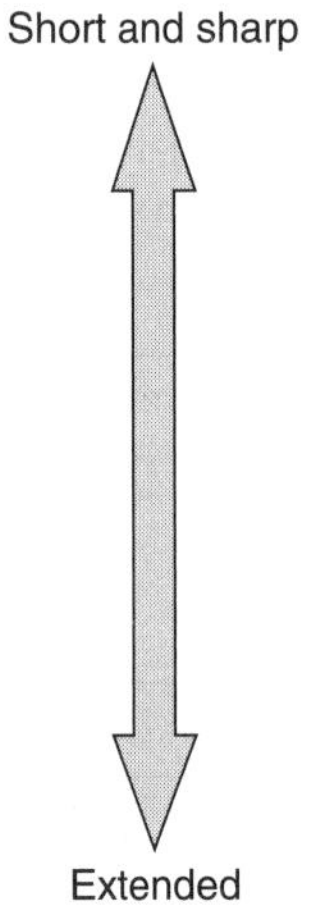

Short and sharp ↑ ↓ Extended

Category	Purpose
Introductions	To learn names and gain confidence by saying something in public
Activities	To learn names, encourage interaction and also promote learning related to the session objectives
Games	To learn names and also encourage interaction between group members

Some suggestions as to the form these might take are:

Introductions
- Learners introduce themselves and write their name on a card or label.
- Each learner interviews someone else and introduces them.
- Sitting in a circle learners throw a ball to each other. Each time it is caught the learner gives their name and an interesting personal fact.

Activities
Activities need to focus on topics related to the subject and are best if these examine learners' previous experience.

- **Snowball:** Consider a chosen topic, for example the best way to study, individually, and then in pairs, then in fours, then feed back to the whole group.

- **Alternate groups:** Learners introduce themselves in a group of four and discuss a given topic. Groups then re-form with learners joining a new group, introducing themselves and reporting the earlier discussion.
- **Expectations:** Learners form small groups, discuss their expectations of the course and report these on flipcharts on which they also write their names.

Games

- **Hello:** A piece of card is cut into four irregular pieces. Each learner is given a piece of card and has to form a group with learners having the three other fitting pieces. Each group then has to find a novel way of saying hello to the rest of the teaching group that includes stating their names.
- **Correct answers:** A question is asked (normally about an opinion) and three possible answers are offered. Learners form groups depending on what they think the answer is and then justify their choice to the rest of the teaching group.
- **Group logo:** Learners are randomly divided into small groups. Each small group devises a logo that includes information about group members.
- **Find a person who:** Learners are given a handout with boxes containing descriptions which might apply to another learner in the group. Examples could be: plays a sport, speaks a language in addition to English, plays a musical instrument, has a birthday in September. Each learner gains information from others until one person has names in all the boxes; then each learner introduces one other learner and one thing they now know about them. You can choose to devise descriptors which relate to your subject area.

There are many alternative icebreakers to choose from and our choice is influenced by factors such as:

- The time available
- The subject matter
- How long the group will be together
- The size and nature of the group.

Your particular teaching situation will determine which of the above are suitable as icebreakers. The icebreaker need not be a lengthy activity but invariably will help to encourage interaction and participation, thus getting the course off to a positive start.

 Activity 2.7

Think about the next group you will meet. Select an appropriate icebreaker to use, either choosing from the list above or devising one of your own. Consider the factors listed above in making your decision.

A positive approach to teaching

We have previously identified actions by the teacher that can have a negative effect on the climate of the course. The following list, although lengthy, is not exhaustive and you may wish to add to it, but it makes a start in identifying **good** practice. These are actions that will help us to promote a positive social and learning environment.

It helps if, when we respond to learners, we:

- ☑ Are enthusiastic and show learners we are interested in them and their work.
- ☑ Provide time and attention for each individual.
- ☑ Treat learners in a consistent manner.
- ☑ Involve learners in the teaching and encourage participation.
- ☑ Give learners opportunities to demonstrate proficiency.

When we provide feedback we:

- ☑ Focus on the positive, not on learners' mistakes.
- ☑ Respond positively to all contributions.
- ☑ Praise at every appropriate opportunity.

When we communicate we:

- ☑ Use positive body language (smiling, eye contact, approving gestures).
- ☑ Use language appropriate to learners.
- ☑ Introduce technical terms with care, use jargon sparingly.
- ☑ Make reference to areas we have in common with learners.
- ☑ Use 'we' whenever possible ('we all agree that …').

It is important that we ensure learners feel comfortable in their learning and feel able to approach us with queries and problems. All of the above make a major contribution to lifting barriers so that very different learners all feel they can participate, contribute and make progress. As we will see in the next chapter, this is a key factor in motivating learners.

Attention to the physical and social environments helps to put our learners in the frame of mind that encourages them to participate fully in the process of communication, through which learning takes place. This process is essential to any teaching session and we next explore how effective communication can create a more successful learning environment.

Chapter summary

- ✓ The learning environment has a physical, social and learning component, each of which has to be managed by the teacher.
- ✓ Communication can be a one-way, two-ways or several-ways process.
- ✓ The way in which the physical and social environments are managed impact upon patterns of communication.
- ✓ First impressions are important in establishing a positive learning environment.
- ✓ Ground rules contribute to effective learning and the setting of these can be led by either teachers or learners.
- ✓ There are a number of ways of 'breaking the ice' and helping groups to gel.

Solution to Activity 2.2

Arrangement 1 Two-way communication
Arrangement 2 One-way communication
Arrangement 3 Several-ways communication

Further reading

Rogers, J. (2007) *Adults Learning* (5th edn). Maidenhead: McGraw-Hill, Open University Press. Written from an adult education perspective, Chapter 2 explores the first meeting between teacher and learners, discussing icebreakers, introductions and helping learners relax.

Useful website

Suggestions for icebreaking activities

http://www.icebreakers.ws/

3

Communicating with learners

Chapter overview

When you have worked through this chapter on communication you will be able to:

- Describe a model of the communication process
- Review the characteristics of effective verbal and non-verbal communication
- Identify potential barriers to communication and how to overcome these

Defining communication

In the last chapter we looked at how we can create a positive learning environment, including the ways in which the physical setting can either encourage or inhibit different patterns of communication. This chapter now focuses on the processes involved in communication with the intention of making communication with our learners more effective.

Communication can be thought of as:

the transfer of information from one person to another with the intention of bringing about a response.

Effective communication – a model

There are many models of communication; their purpose is to help us understand the process more easily. The simplest is illustrated below:

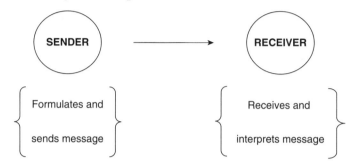

This could suggest that communication involves one person talking to another, who listens and takes in what is being said. This often happens in our teaching sessions when we are giving instructions or explanations. We use our voice to communicate. We all have different voices – some loud, some soft, some high, some low, some have distinct accents. Some of us like the sound of them; others do not. Whatever our voice, we can make the most of it by considering the following:

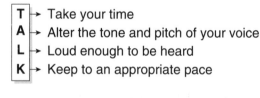

T ⟩ Take your time

Although we will be looking at pace of delivery later, it is worth remembering that whatever we say is more effective if we have thought it through, even if only briefly. Sometimes a slightly slower delivery or pause for thought can make a considerable difference as it allows us to 'engage brain before opening mouth'.

We all recognise the importance of the pause in everyday communication, but as teachers we do not always use it to best effect in teaching. Great communicators understand 'the art of the pause'. We may be feeling a little nervous and consequently not inclined to pause, as this may invite questions that we would prefer to avoid. If such feelings can be overcome, pauses can be used to good effect, provided they are not too long or used too frequently. Think back to teaching sessions in which you have been involved or even conversations you have had with friends. How were pauses used?

 ## Activity 3.1

Identify ways in which you have heard pauses being used to good effect.

You may have considered the following:

- Pausing before speaking or answering a question allows us to gather our thoughts and formulate a clearer response
- Pausing allows the learner or group to prepare to receive our response
- Pausing during instructing or explaining allows us to emphasise key points
- Pausing allows our learners to absorb a number of consecutive points
- Pausing after instructing, explaining or supplying the answer to a question signals that the point has now been dealt with and we are moving on to a new area.

A ⟩ Alter the tone and pitch of your voice

Sometimes a teacher's voice is described as boring or monotonous. This can lead to loss of attention or in extreme cases learners have been known to fall asleep! We can avoid this by varying the tone and pitch of our voices. When we are in conversation our voices become animated, rising and falling subconsciously, probably because conversations tend to be spontaneous. We plan and may rehearse our teaching, however, and this often leads to a more measured and flat delivery.

Sounds that are designed to capture attention (sirens on police cars and ambulances for instance) vary, altering their tone and pitch. We should try and remember this when teaching and use it to our advantage.

L ⟩ Loud enough to be heard

We do not have difficulty in judging how loud our voice should be when talking with a friend. We automatically adjust to our surroundings, whether we are in a quiet or a noisy room, next to each other or some distance apart. As the number of people we are talking to increases this becomes more difficult. This is why it can be hard for us to judge the appropriate volume level for our voice when teaching.

Sometimes we need help with this and it is not uncommon for teachers to ask if they can be heard at the back of the room. The volume we are looking for is reached when everyone can hear but it is not uncomfortably loud. Rather than ask our learners if they can hear, we can achieve an appropriate volume in a teaching environment by focusing on the learners at the back of the room and talking to them. This has the effect of achieving a volume that suits all the learners in the room. Sometimes, however, we may choose to use a quieter voice to good effect in order to give emphasis to the point we are making.

K ⟩ Keep to an appropriate pace

In deciding on an appropriate pace we will need to bear a number of factors in mind.

In the next Activity box you are asked to identify factors which you think have an influence on your pace of delivery.

 Activity 3.2

What do you consider affects the pace of your delivery?

Our normal speaking rate is about 140 words per minute and this is manageable for most listeners. If we talk faster than this, learners will find it hard work to process the information. If, on the other hand, we talk more slowly we may well lose their attention.

The previous knowledge and experience of our learners will have a bearing on the rate at which they can receive and process information. If we are communicating new and fairly complex information, learners will need more time to process and file it away (even with appropriate use of pauses), and so a slower pace is required. If we are communicating information with which they have some familiarity, or the information is simple or less important, merely providing background or repetition, our pace of delivery can be quicker.

Pace of delivery is also affected by other factors, such as the number of learners we are addressing. How confident we feel about our material and the time available to us will also have an effect on the pacing of delivery.

An awareness of all these factors will help us determine the most appropriate pace of delivery. To check this, we need to note the response that learners are making and this is where 'non–verbal' cues play an important part. We shall be looking at these in the following pages.

So, we communicate with learners by talking to them. Similarly, they talk to us. Therefore, both listening and talking are important skills in the communication process. Our model of communication has now become a little more complex.

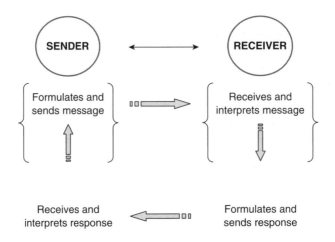

We are now considering communication to be a two-way process involving listening as well as talking. Listening involves:

- Clearing the mind ready to receive the message
- Focusing on what is being said rather than thinking about our reply
- Checking that our interpretation is correct.

To make communication productive, both parties need to recognise that each is participating fully. It is easy to know when someone is talking as we can hear the words, but how do we know when someone is listening?

 Activity 3.3

What makes you consider that someone is listening to you?

We need to regard listening as an *active* process, in which signals are sent to the other person to let them know we are listening.

Active listening is recognised by a range of non-verbal cues such as:

- Eye contact
- Head nodding
- Leaning forward
- Alert facial expressions
- Open body language.

Verbally, we show active listening largely through a technique known as summarising.

This involves phrases such as....

Active listening, then, shows the learner that we are interested in what they have to say. This helps to promote the climate of openness and trust that is important to establish effective communication.

Non-verbal communication

So far we have largely explored communication that uses the spoken word, but it can be argued that although we speak with our voices, we communicate with our whole body, as has been seen in active listening.

Simple things like whether we stand or sit to address our learners, our posture and the expression on our face, all send messages that play as important a role in the communication process as the words we use. Such non-verbal signals have a significant effect on the way in which our learners receive and interpret messages. These must now be added to our model of the communication process.

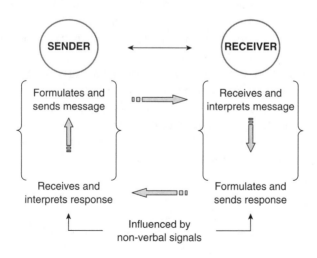

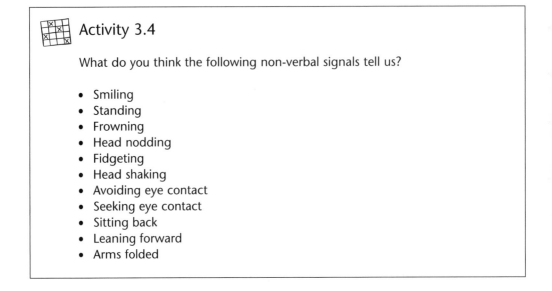

Activity 3.4

What do you think the following non-verbal signals tell us?

- Smiling
- Standing
- Frowning
- Head nodding
- Fidgeting
- Head shaking
- Avoiding eye contact
- Seeking eye contact
- Sitting back
- Leaning forward
- Arms folded

Interpreting non-verbal communication can be difficult, particularly as different cues can have a variety of interpretations depending on the cultural context, but it does add another important dimension to our understanding of the communication process.

From the learner's perspective, our smiles, posture, demeanour and appearance contribute much to our acceptance, rapport and initial credibility. All of these can therefore influence how our message is received.

We often use our hands to help interpretation and to give emphasis, but perhaps the most important aspect of non-verbal communication is eye contact. In normal conversation we would expect to maintain a considerable degree of eye contact. Indeed, avoiding eye contact would give the conversation an uncomfortable or awkward feel. When we talk to a group of people, however, eye contact with each individual is far less frequent, but remains just as significant and important to the success of the communication process.

A lack of eye contact when we teach can be interpreted as a lack of confidence on our part. It can lead to learners not feeling part of what is going on; attention and involvement can subsequently decrease. It is important therefore, when we are engaged in teaching that we make a conscious effort to make eye contact with everyone in the group. This will have the effect of making everyone feel part of the communication process; it helps us to judge understanding and decide on the pacing of activities.

Barriers to communication

So far, we have considered the positive aspects of non-verbal communication, but sometimes it can provide a distraction and take attention away from the information being communicated. If we are nervous, for instance, our arms and hands seem to become larger and more obvious. What do we do with them when we are not using them to help interpretation or provide emphasis? We could, perhaps, run our fingers through our hair, straighten our clothes, play with watches, rings, or loose change, or stroke our necks or foreheads. All of these provide distractions that hinder the communication process. Anything that interferes with getting the message across is termed a barrier to communication, which we should seek to avoid.

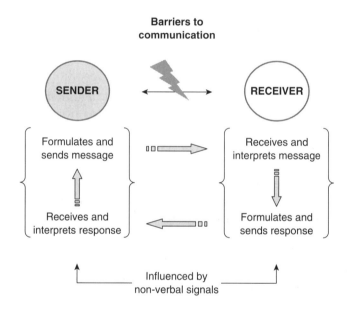

Distractions caused by the non-verbal communications of the teacher are just one type of barrier.

Activity 3.5

Identify any potential barriers to communication in your teaching context.

The barriers you have identified will depend on your previous experience; for example, someone who is hearing impaired and needs to lip read may find a moustache which masks lip movement a major barrier to communication. Whatever your previous experience the barriers will probably fall into one of the categories below:

External barriers

- **Physical** – noise, interruptions, discomfort (hot, airless, cold, too light or dark, poor acoustics)
- **Language** – strong accent or dialect, technical language, other jargon
- **Relevance** – too theoretical, no relationship to learners' experience or role
- **Lack of rapport** – with teacher, other learners

It is within our power as teachers to deal with the problems caused by many of the external barriers. We can alter seating arrangements to accommodate more participation. We can minimise the effects of noise and interruptions. We can try to adjust heat and light to appropriate levels. We can introduce relevant practical examples whenever possible rather than use technical terms or jargon.

We can also take care with language ensuring that neither we nor our learners give offence. Language or terms that contain negative overtones relating to race, gender, culture, sexual orientation, age or disability should be avoided and more positive words and phrases used.

We can establish rapport using icebreakers. Sometimes, however, the barriers are difficult for us to identify as, rather than being caused by the teaching environment, they may be internal barriers, personal to learners.

Internal barriers

- **Psychological** – preoccupation with other matters, lack of interest or confidence
- **Past experience** – preconceived ideas, dislike of learning methods, stereotyping
- **Resistance to change** – dislike of something new
- **Personal** – mistrust of teacher, teacher's motives, prejudice

Internal barriers are much more difficult to deal with than external barriers. We may not even be aware of them, although their effects may well be apparent.

The first step in dealing with internal barriers is to identify them. This is unlikely to happen unless we have created an appropriate social and learning environment, as described in the last chapter. The most common internal barriers we encounter as teachers are related to learner motivation and we shall look at this in the next chapter.

Chapter summary

The main points covered in this chapter are:

- ✓ Effective use of the voice depends upon a number of factors.
- ✓ Active listening is an important aspect of the communication process.
- ✓ Communication can be non-verbal as well as verbal.
- ✓ Barriers to communication can be both external and internal.

Further reading

Jaques, D. and Salmon, G. (2007) *Learning in Groups: A Handbook for Face-to-Face and Online Environments* (4th edn) London: Routledge.
See Chapter 4 of this book for a very readable discussion of communication, barriers to communication and giving feedback.

Siddons, S. (2008) *The Complete Presentation Skills Handbook*. London: Kogan Page.
Although this is not a book specifically about teaching, you may want to look at Chapter 10, 'Voice and Performance Skills', and Chapter 11, 'Nerves and Body Language'.

Useful websites

Active listening

  http://toolboxes.flexiblelearning.net.au/demosites/series2/205/SEGMENTS/INTCLNTS/Actvlist.htm

Non-verbal communication

  http://nonverbal.ucsc.edu/

Voice projection

  http://www.triadpublishing.com/speakers.shtml

4

Motivating learners and managing behaviour

Chapter overview

When you have worked through this chapter on motivation and managing behaviour you will be able to:

- Distinguish between intrinsic and extrinsic motivation
- List strategies that may be used to increase learner motivation
- Describe approaches to behaviour management which use rewards and sanctions
- Identify the role of self-concept in causing inappropriate behaviour
- Describe ways of changing self-concept from a negative to a positive perspective
- Differentiate between aggressive, passive and assertive responses to inappropriate behaviour

Motivation

Each time we meet a new group of lifelong learners, the only certainty that we can rely on is that they will all have their own particular needs, characteristics and peculiarities. They will all be individuals in their own right. It is coping with this range of different personalities and aptitudes, and helping individuals learn and form as a group, that makes teaching in the lifelong learning sector both challenging and rewarding.

Although the learners themselves are different, they all go through a similar process in their learning. This allows general principles to be identified that can guide us in making learning more effective. Generally, learning is more effective when:

1   We are motivated to want to learn
2   We can focus and hold attention on the material we are learning
3   We readily understand the material
4   The material is presented in a format that matches our natural learning style
5   We can hold the material in our memory
6   We can use what we have learned in real-life situations
7   We feel valued and acknowledged by others in the learning environment.

Of the areas outlined above, motivation is a key issue, as without it, it is unlikely that learners will progress. There are various theories of motivation which seem to fall into one of two main categories.

One view of motivation considers it to be a process that is controlled by factors in our immediate environment. These factors are external to us as a person and so the term used to express this viewpoint is **extrinsic** motivation.

The opposing view regards our own internal needs to be the controlling factor as these are what drive or motivate us to do what we do. This type of motivation is termed **intrinsic** motivation.

Extrinsic factors include qualifications, a pay rise, the approval of others, meeting other people, promotion, praise, and, last but by no means least, the model of enthusiasm provided by the teacher, regardless of the particular subject to be covered, group to be taught or time of day.

Extrinsic motivation is an area on which we as teachers can have an effect. Extrinsic motivators after all, come from the environment and as teachers we are managers of the learning environment. Although some extrinsic motivators, such as pay rises and promotion, are not within our control, there are plenty of other options open to us.

Some relate to the teacher and their actions

☑ Present an enthusiastic role model.
☑ Be professional but approachable.
☑ Make learners feel they matter.
☑ Use praise freely, but only when deserved.
☑ Give constructive, positive feedback.

Others are concerned with the environment

☑ Provide appropriate facilities and conditions.
☑ Create a supportive environment where everyone feels part of the group.
☑ Set a relaxed but purposeful atmosphere in which mistakes are not ridiculed.
☑ Communicate using a range of media that suit each learner's needs.

Others relate to the way in which teaching sessions are conducted

☑ Give learners the opportunity to participate in setting their own goals.
☑ Set tasks that are challenging but achievable.
☑ Encourage active participation in the session.

A much-quoted model of motivation is that of Maslow (1943), which is summarised below and related to the teaching and learning context. Maslow considers motivation to be intrinsic. Individuals are driven by inner needs, some of which are identified here. Maslow maintains that some of these needs take priority over others – they exist in a hierarchy.

The order of satisfying these needs starts at the bottom of the list and works its way up to the top, so needs of the body (physiological) take precedence over all of the others and achieving individual potential (self-actualisation) is only addressed when all of the needs below it in the list have been satisfied.

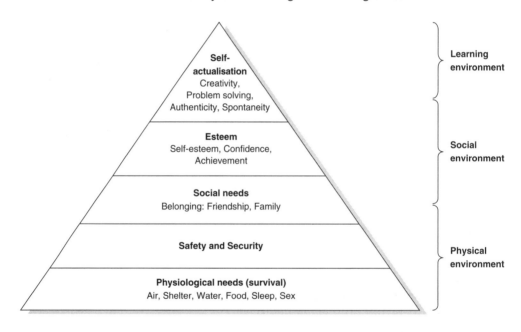

Maslow's hierarchy in a teaching and learning context

Looking back at Chapter 2 on setting an appropriate environment, it can be seen that Physiological and Safety needs are part of the physical environment, Social and Esteem needs fall within the social environment and Self-actualisation is what is strived for in the learning environment. Maslow confirms then that there is a need to address the physical and social environments before motivation is focused on learning. More importantly for our present discussion, Maslow suggests that what motivates learners is the internal need to achieve their potential.

Generally, intrinsic motivators such as the need to self-actualise are more powerful motivators than extrinsic motivators. Intrinsic motivators are also more effective in bringing about learning as they focus on the actual learning itself rather than what results from it or the context in which it is set.

Some of our learners are intrinsically motivated when we first meet them and have a clear aim to achieve their individual potential; the task then is to maintain their motivation at that level. Others, however, may not be motivated in this way and so the task here is not to maintain but to foster intrinsic motivation.

If doctors wish to treat an ailment they must first of all know what is causing it, to arrive at the most appropriate treatment strategy. The same applies to motivation. If we wish to bring about motivation in learners, we can decide how to go about this if we have some idea of the reasons for its initial absence.

 **Activity 4.1**

List some of the reasons why learners may be demotivated in a learning situation.

Your list is probably quite lengthy as there are many potential reasons for learners being demotivated. Perhaps motivation has been blunted by lack of success in previous experiences of learning or it may be that attendance is not voluntary.

Activity 4.2

Revisit the reasons you have listed above. Pick out three of these and then identify strategies you could use to improve the situation in each case. You may find it useful to refer back to the list of extrinsic motivators to help you in this task.

We can affect motivation, then, by working on extrinsic factors with the intention that, as time progresses, these will bring about a shift towards intrinsic motivation. If learners come on your course to achieve qualifications, for instance, you can boost their motivation by being enthusiastic yourself; giving your approval through praise and by showing them they are succeeding. This will encourage your learners to gradually become more interested in the content and enjoy learning and so motivation is progressively internalised.

Approaches to behaviour management

Teachers consider the management of motivation to be an important skill, since high levels of motivation are key to effective learning. Conversely, low levels of motivation make learning less likely but, more seriously, can lead to difficult or challenging behaviours on the part of some learners.

Activity 4.3

What behaviours might you consider as difficult or challenging?

It is unlikely that you will have noted many, if any, examples of serious confrontation between learners and teachers or open challenges to the teacher's authority. Your examples are more likely to fall into the category of what two reports on school discipline (The Elton Report, 1989; The Steer Report, 2005) call 'low level disruption'.

Low level disruption can be thought of as any form of behaviour that prevents teachers teaching or learners learning, and typically includes learners:

- Persistently talking to each other
- Distracting others from their work
- Making unnecessary (non-verbal) noise
- Fooling around (for example throwing paper aeroplanes)
- Asking inappropriate questions
- Using mobile phones and texting
- Reading magazines or newspapers
- 'Winding up' the teacher
- Withdrawing completely from the session.

Whilst none of these might be considered as extremely serious in themselves, the cumulative effects can be draining for teachers. These events are significant because they disturb the flow of the session and interfere with learning. Over a period of time such behaviours, if not addressed, can create a climate in which the likelihood of more serious incidents is increased.

We have seen the diverse nature of lifelong learning and learners in Chapter 1: the vast majority of our learners are unlikely to pose such problems. The remainder of this chapter, therefore, needs to be read and interpreted within the perspective of your own particular working context and adapted as necessary.

There are two general views of inappropriate behaviour:

- The behaviours themselves are the problem and must be dealt with directly.
- The behaviours are ways of highlighting an underlying problem and it is the cause of this problem that must be identified and dealt with, leading to the disappearance of the symptoms.

Neither view will generate successful strategies if we do not consider ourselves as role models in interactions, jointly contributing to solutions we would like to see.

If you subscribe to the first view of inappropriate behaviour your strategies will revolve around rules, rewards and sanctions. We have already referred to ground rules and the different ways of arriving at these in Chapter 2. The setting of rules is a common approach to regulating behaviour.

Rules play a key role in 'assertive discipline' approaches in which learners are encouraged to choose to behave in an appropriate manner through a system of rewards and consequences. Assertive discipline consists of three parts:

1 A number of rules (usually about five – the fewer rules the more effective the approach) that are to be followed at all times by all learners, who are fully aware of what they are.
2 A system of awarding positive recognition to all learners following the rules.
3 A series of consequences that follow a choice not to follow the rules. The level of consequence is proportional to the severity or frequency of rule breaking and again all learners are fully aware of these consequences.

You can find out more about this approach by following up the suggested reading and web links at the end of the chapter.

To understand the second view of inappropriate behaviour we need to identify the reasons behind the behaviours that concern us.

Activity 4.4

What do you think the reasons are for the behaviours you identified in Activity 4.3?

The causes of challenging behaviour can range from boredom to testing the teacher's resolve and ability to maintain order; from diverting attention from feelings of inadequacy to 'having a laugh'; from conforming to group norms to maintaining a sense of individuality.

Self-concept

Of particular interest is the notion of diverting attention from feelings of inadequacy. Psychology tells us that we all have a particular way of thinking of ourselves – our self-concept. This consists of two parts: self-image, which is the more fact-based 'self-portrait' we have of ourselves; and self-esteem, which is concerned with the worth or value that we place upon ourselves. Our self-concepts are shaped by our previous experience and the responses and feedback we experience 'in the moment'. These influence and shape the way we behave. To some extent, self-concept is also dependent on the context within which we find ourselves. You might be the life and soul of the party talking to friends in an informal setting, for instance, but be terrified of giving a talk to a group of strangers.

The self-concept we exhibit in a learning environment is often known as the 'academic' self-concept. Suppose you have a positive academic self-concept; your previous experiences of learning are of success and you therefore expect a similar outcome in your current learning. You know that if you try hard and show a positive attitude towards your work you are likely to reap the rewards of your efforts. Your energy will thus be channelled into your work rather than inappropriate behaviour.

If, on the other hand, you have a negative academic self-concept, the picture is rather different. In a learning situation you will expect to experience difficulty or perhaps ultimately fail altogether. You will feel anxious and unsure of yourself. Your main aim will be to avoid further failure and, for you, applying yourself to the work in hand does not achieve this.

You do have a number of other strategies you can resort to, however. You can blame your teacher for your failure; you can withdraw from the lesson or engage in a number of avoidance techniques such as not bringing pens, pencils or any necessary equipment to the session. If pushed to work you can simply refuse, as the consequences of refusal are preferable to the consequences of failure. All of these strategies can be perceived as, or lead to, challenging behaviour.

Developing a positive self-concept

Lifelong learning is often referred to as 'the second chance', and so a proportion of learners we encounter may well have a background of previous lack of educational success. If we subscribe to the second view of inappropriate behaviour, our efforts will be less concerned with behaviour itself, focusing more on bringing about a positive academic self-concept, thus removing the need for the learner to behave in a challenging manner.

 Activity 4.5

What strategies could you use to bring about a positive change in academic self-concept?

As one of the key causes of negative self-concept in a learner is lack of success, your responses to the above activity will no doubt be largely concerned with achieving success in learning and recognising such successes. This may be achieved through:

☑ Setting regular short-term goals.
☑ Agreeing individual targets which are challenging but achievable.
☑ Making learning active.
☑ Ensuring learners know exactly what is to be achieved and why.
☑ Breaking tasks down into shorter, manageable 'chunks'.
☑ Starting with simpler, straightforward tasks and gradually increasing the complexity.
☑ Creating time for more one-to-one contact.
☑ Looking for the positives in learners' work.
☑ Showing that you expect them to be successful.
☑ Encouraging learners to reflect and build upon their successes.
☑ Recording and pointing out progress.
☑ Using praise to acknowledge success.

And, most important of all:

☑ Listening to what learners have to say.

Responses to inappropriate behaviour

These two views of behaviour provide different ways of approaching the problems posed by challenging behaviour in the teaching situation. There will be occasions when we need to tackle behaviour directly; for example when it constitutes a health and safety risk. There will be other times when we will be looking for a longer-term solution by tackling the root cause of the behaviour. Effective behaviour management invariably involves a combination of each approach in appropriate measures.

Some groups will contain higher proportions than others of learners exhibiting challenging behaviour. Interestingly, however, not all individuals or groups demonstrate the same degree of inappropriate behaviour with all of their teachers. Some 14–16 year olds in a college environment revealed the following thoughts about who were considered to be 'good' teachers, for whom they behaved well.

Clearly, the relationship between teacher and learners is important, but reaching an understanding of what is being taught and a sense of having achieved something also play their part. Although these views are expressed by 14–16 year-olds, they could equally well apply to your learners or to any learner within the sector.

Normally, learners will not present difficult behaviour if they feel that they are valued and are getting something from the session, so teachers who themselves behave appropriately and who create a positive learning environment (refer back to Chapter 2) are less likely to encounter difficult behaviour from their learners.

Various studies have come to the conclusion that good classroom management, accompanied by good interpersonal skills, is key in pre-empting difficult behaviour – 'nipping it in the bud' before it becomes serious. Effective practice in this area can include the following:

Beginning sessions

> ☑ Be in the room first, greet learners individually, if possible, making good eye contact.
> ☑ Attitude is important – if you show that you are pleased to be there, perhaps they will be as well!
> ☑ Have a 'starter' activity ready, giving an active and purposeful beginning.
> ☑ Show you are well prepared and confident.
> ☑ Explain simply but clearly what is to be achieved in the session and why it will be useful.

During sessions

> ☑ Make sure learners are occupied throughout the session in relevant and sufficiently challenging activities.
> ☑ Make sure that activities are clearly explained and have a purpose.
> ☑ Expect a definite 'end product' to an activity and make sure learners are aware of time limits, without creating too much pressure.
> ☑ Use a differentiated approach so all are engaged in stretching but achievable work.
> ☑ Maintain the momentum of the session – try to avoid periods of inactivity, no matter how short.
> ☑ Think where best to position yourself in the room at different stages of the session; the more confidently you move around the room and interact with learners, the less confrontational the situation is likely to be.
> ☑ Show you are aware of potential problems and deal with them quickly before they can escalate.

Ending sessions

> ☑ Leave sufficient time for an ordered ending to the session.
> ☑ Acknowledge the learning that has taken place.
> ☑ Identify progress and give praise if appropriate.

Smith and Laslett (1993) have devised 'four rules of classroom management', and in these suggest that, of the above stages, it is the management of the beginnings and endings of sessions that is crucial in maintaining good order.

Sometimes, however, more serious instances of challenging behaviour can occur and these need to be handled appropriately to defuse matters and prevent an escalation of the situation. Sometimes it is not so much what we do that is the biggest influence in these situations, but rather how we do it. It is not what we say to the learner who is being difficult, but the manner in which we say it that matters the most. Emotions can run high on both sides in any form of confrontation and play their part in affecting the outcome. Consider the following activity:

Activity 4.6

What feelings might be aroused in teachers when confronted with a challenge to their authority?

Whenever we are faced by a situation we perceive as threatening, adrenalin is released into the body, readying it to respond to the perceived threat by fighting or running away. This is known as the fight-or-flight response. A fight response is accompanied by feelings of anger, flight by feelings of apprehension. It is this emotional reaction that determines how we subsequently act.

If a teacher feels angry when faced with a perceived challenge to their authority, their reaction is likely to be aggressive. The language used would be characterised by:

- Criticism – 'can't you get it right even after I've explained it to you twice?'
- Sarcasm – 'even my grandmother knows that'
- Blunt refusals – 'of course you can't do that'
- Strong commands – 'I won't tell you again, just stop that now!'
- Grudging praise – 'well I suppose it's better than your last effort'

and would be accompanied by aggressive body language and tone of voice.

Activity 4.7

If you are addressed in an aggressive manner, how does it make you feel and how are you likely to react?

Acting aggressively will invariably provoke a similarly aggressive response from the learner, and soon the situation becomes more confrontational and can spiral out of control.

If, on the other hand, apprehension is the primary emotion aroused, the teacher will offer a much more passive reaction. The type of language used in this instance would be characterised by:

- An inability to say 'no' – 'perhaps it's best if you don't do that just now'
- Avoidance of direct instruction – 'now it might be a good idea if you waited till after break'
- Avoidance of direct criticism – 'personally I think it's quite good but I don't think the examiner would agree'
- Allocating blame – 'I know it's quite soon to hand in work but the Course Leader set that date'

and again accompanied by corresponding tone of voice and body language.

Activity 4.8

If you are addressed in a passive manner, how does it make you feel and how would you react?

A passive reaction from the teacher can leave learners confused, lacking in direction and ultimately more frustrated than they were to start with. They can feel that the teacher is not sufficiently concerned to make a commitment.

Quite often then, if we act from the emotion of the moment, the ways in which we handle difficult situations can be counterproductive. Watkins (1997) suggests a sequence of:

1 **Feel:** Initial emotive reaction
2 **Think:** Refer back to previous experience and knowledge
3 **Do:** Now decide on and carry through a course of action.

The examples above illustrate *Feel* and *Do*, missing out the second stage of *Think*; Watkins refers to this combination as *reacting*. He suggests that it is far more productive to complete the whole sequence, thus *responding* rather than reacting. If we respond, we are basing our actions around a rational rather than emotional backdrop. Our state of mind is calm rather than angry or apprehensive and so our response is assertive.

It is important that we learn to be emotionally self-aware and manage our own behaviours and relationships appropriately. All social interactions are a shared responsibility and we need to recognise our own role in generating learner reactions.

The type of language used in an assertive response can be characterised by:

- Clear instructions with reasons – 'I want you to sit down now as you are distracting others from their work'
- Saying no but with reasons – 'you can't do it that way as it might catch fire'
- Encouraging learners to express themselves – 'you say you disagree but what exactly are your reasons for this?'
- Including praise when offering criticism – 'although you haven't produced much work, you started off really well'

once more accompanied by corresponding tone of voice and body language.

Activity 4.9

If you were addressed in an assertive manner, how would it make you feel and what would your likely reaction be?

Assertive responses can defuse difficult situations.

There are a number of techniques associated with assertiveness, and a summary of these can be found on the websites listed at the end of the chapter.

In this chapter we have looked at some aspects of dealing with inappropriate behaviours. Our review aims to give you some ideas against which to examine your own practice and suggests further avenues to explore.

As a final thought, here are some reflections on their own practice by a group of teachers who teach 'disaffected' learners. Perhaps they contain good advice regardless of who our learners are.

- We try not to be confrontational
- We encourage learners to take responsibility for their own behaviour
- We have ground rules – ideally set by learners
- We always act promptly at the first sign of trouble
- We sometimes get down to their level
- We nag (because I want you to succeed)
- We give occasional incentives
- We give learners choices whenever we can
- We listen to learners and generally aim to be approachable.

Chapter summary

✓ Motivation can be internal to learners (intrinsic) or come from an outside source (extrinsic).
✓ Maslow's Hierarchy of Needs is a model of intrinsic motivation.
✓ As teachers, we use methods of extrinsic motivation to promote intrinsic motivation in learners.
✓ Inappropriate behaviour can be managed by strategies such as setting ground rules and 'assertive discipline'.
✓ A poor 'academic self-concept' can lead to difficult or challenging behaviour.
✓ Strategies aimed at improving self-concept result in improved behaviour.
✓ Effective classroom management can prevent inappropriate behaviour.
✓ Aggressive or passive reactions to challenging behaviour can lead to escalation. Assertive responses can defuse difficult situations.

→ References

The Elton Report (1989) *Discipline in Schools: Report of the Committee of Enquiry, chaired by Lord Elton*. London: HMSO.

Maslow, A.H. (1943) 'A Theory of Human Motivation', *Psychological Review* 50: 370–96.

Smith, C. and Laslett, R. (1993) *Effective Classroom Management: A Teacher's Guide*. London: Routledge.

The Steer Report (2005) *Learning Behaviour: The Report of The Practitioners' Group on School Behaviour and Discipline, chaired by Sir Alan Steer*. London: DfES.

Watkins, C. (1997) *Managing Classroom Behaviour*. London: Association of Teachers and Lecturers.

📖 Further reading

Vizard, D. (2007) *How to Manage Behaviour in Further Education*. London: Paul Chapman Publishing.
A user friendly approach which looks specifically at Further Education and 14–16 in particular. Practical rather than theoretical, covering all aspects of difficult behaviour, it comes complete with a CD of Staff Development exercises.

Wallace, S. (2007) *Managing Behaviour in the Lifelong Learning Sector* (2nd edn). Exeter: Learning Matters.
Written for the lifelong learning sector, this looks at motivation and behaviour in a commonsense manner. Contains lots of case studies for analysis and reflection.

🖱 Useful websites

Assertive discipline

Article by Lee Canter on the background to the approach and some of the issues it raises
http://campus.dyc.edu/~drwaltz/FoundLearnTheory/FLT_readings/Canter.htm
Article from the TES on 'mistakes teachers make' regarding behaviour management
http://www.tes.co.uk/article.aspx?storycode=6000095

5

Starting to plan

Chapter overview

When you have worked through this chapter on planning you will be able to:

- Identify the reasons for planning teaching
- List the factors to be taken into consideration when planning sessions
- Identify the sequence of planning decisions involved in the teaching cycle
- Define and distinguish between aims and learning objectives
- Write clear aims and learning objectives for sessions
- Identify factors influencing your choice of method
- Identify a range of learning methods and select appropriate methods

Why plan? All the chapters in this book start with a box outlining what you will be able to do upon completion. Read the box at the top of this page again; you now have a clear idea of what you will be covering in this chapter. The contents of the box are the 'learning objectives' or 'learning outcomes' for this chapter. The two terms can be defined differently but are often used interchangeably, so for the sake of simplicity we will stick to the term 'learning objective'.

We found it helpful, in writing this book, to decide on the intended 'learning objectives' prior to developing each chapter. Before we could consider what should be included in this chapter on planning for teaching, *we* needed to decide what *you* should be able to do in order to be successful in planning and preparing your teaching sessions. Until we had made this decision, we could not start to think about appropriate content, activities and checks on learning. You will also find this systematic approach useful in your own planning.

This chapter focuses on the process of planning in general and specifically on the decisions you will make prior to delivering any form of teaching. These decisions are recorded on a written plan (see Chapter 13 for detail and formats). When you have worked through this chapter, you should be able to develop plans for your own sessions that will make clear:

- What you are trying to achieve – the learning objective(s).

In future chapters we will look at:

- What methods you will select
- What resources you will choose
- How you will assess and then review what you have done.

Before we begin to examine the decisions on which we base our planning, we must first appreciate *why* we plan. As you will realise, professionals in the lifelong learning sector lead busy lives with little enough time to fulfil all of the roles and responsibilities discussed in Chapter 1. Why spend precious time devising plans for teaching sessions? What are the advantages?

If we plan and prepare something first, whatever we do will be more effective and, in the long term, will save us time. If we write out a list before we go shopping, for instance, we are more likely to come back with all the things we need. Similarly, if you write a session plan you are more likely to conduct your teaching in an organised and systematic manner.

What to consider in planning

In the same way that a shopping list records decisions we make before we go shopping, a session plan is a record of all the decisions we will have to make before teaching. Deciding what to include on a shopping list is quite easy. We decide what meals to make, we look in our kitchen to see which ingredients we already have, note which items are missing and then we write our list. What to include in a session plan is not as straightforward. There are many more factors to think about and decide upon.

 Activity 5.1

What do you think you will have to consider as part of planning a teaching session?

Perhaps you included some or all of the following:

- Length of the session
- Time of day
- Room/venue
- Individual learners' prior knowledge and experience
- Individual support needs
- Size and mix of group
- Learning objectives
- Content
- Teaching notes
- Visual aids
- Other resources or materials
- Any health and safety concerns
- Teaching methods
- Activities for learners
- External requirements
- How to check learning has occurred.

This is quite an extensive list. Which item do we consider first? Is there a logical order? How do we record everything on a plan?

The sequence in planning

In the last activity, when you thought about the factors to consider prior to teaching, did you think of things in any particular order or did they just tumble onto the page? Is there a set order in which to think about these factors or might the order be different each time you plan?

Consider the following: when you are going on holiday you will find there are a lot of decisions to be made. We have listed some of them below:

- Which clothes will you take?
- How will you get there?
- Where will you go?
- How much money will you need?
- Where will you stay?

Activity 5.2

Put the holiday decisions above into a logical order.

You will probably agree with the order below:

1 Where to go
2 Where to stay
3 How to get there
4 What money to take
5 Which clothes to take.

We have chosen this order because until you have decided where you want to go, you cannot make an informed decision about the remaining travel arrangements. You will feel rather silly, for instance, if you decide first on clothes to take (swimsuit, sunglasses), how to get there (by train) and then decide to go to Alaska. If going to Alaska is your starting point, then it is easy to decide how to get there; you want to get there quickly and so you will fly. You can now decide what money and which clothes to take.

As you can see, there is a logical sequence in making these holiday decisions; a similar logic applies to the decisions you make before teaching.

Holiday decisions	Teaching decisions
1 Where will I go?	1 What is to be learned?
2 How will I get there?	2 What methods are to be used?
3 What will I take?	3 What resources are appropriate?

If you go on holiday to a new destination, you need to know if you have arrived at the right place. You will want to check, 'Am I at the Hotel Iceberg in Alaska?'

Later on, back home, you may think about returning for a future holiday. This decision would be based on looking back over your recent experience and seeing if you thought everything went well. Did you like the scenery? Was it easy to get to? How was the accommodation? Next time you might decide not to go to Alaska, or to visit Alaska but stay in another hotel, based upon your experiences of this year.

When we conduct any form of teaching we also need to know if we have reached our destination. Have our learners achieved what we wanted them to? We would also think about whether we would teach in this way again. We might change the session totally next time or adjust it. We now have two further stages to add to our sequence:

Holiday decisions	Teaching decisions
1 Where will I go?	1 What is to be learned?
2 How will I get there?	2 What methods are to be used?
3 What will I take?	3 What resources are appropriate?
4 How will I check I have reached the correct destination?	4 How is learning to be checked?
5 Was this a good holiday? Would I do it again?	5 What changes (if any) would I make to this session if I were to do it again?

We now have a sequence of decisions to make before we engage in the planning of any teaching. Before we can start to make these decisions, however, we need to consider the needs that have to be met by the teaching we plan. We will want to ask questions about the needs of:

- The syllabus/curriculum/award body
- The teacher (ourselves)
- The learners.

Considering these will help us decide the form and content of the teaching, but in terms of the actual delivery, the learners and their needs are our first consideration.

Activity 5.3

What characteristics of learners might need to be taken into account in planning a teaching session?

You will have identified a number of reasons why learners might be our first consideration; perhaps the proof of this is in the fact that no two teaching sessions are the same. Although the same learning may be involved, we modify each session to respond to the particular group we are teaching. This is because the learners are different each time and we need to take these differences into account. Differences in learners may relate to characteristics such as motivation, previous experience, personality, gender, age and other factors that we will consider in a later chapter.

If we consider learner characteristics beforehand, we can make decisions tailored to the needs of specific groups and focus our teaching more effectively. Sometimes you will not meet your learners until the time of teaching, but the more you can find out about them in advance, the more informed your planning decisions will be.

We have now identified all the key considerations we need to take into account in our teaching; the full sequence of planning decisions is summarised below:

Decisions	What we do
Who are our learners?	Analyse learners' **needs**
What is it we are trying to teach?	Write teaching **aims**
What is to be learned?	Write **learning objectives**
How is learning to take place?	Decide on **methods**/learning activities
What is needed to assist learning?	Identify **resources**
How will the learning be identified?	Decide on how to **assess** learning
How would this session be modified in the future?	Select methods to **evaluate** the session

The specific teaching terms that appear in the second column of the diagram above will be dealt with in more detail as you progress through the book. If you would like a brief definition of these terms at this stage, please refer to the glossary at the back of the book.

The decisions above have been presented as a list, but you will notice that the outcome of the last decision will inform the whole planning process next time around. It is therefore useful to view the planning process as a cycle with each particular stage informing the next.

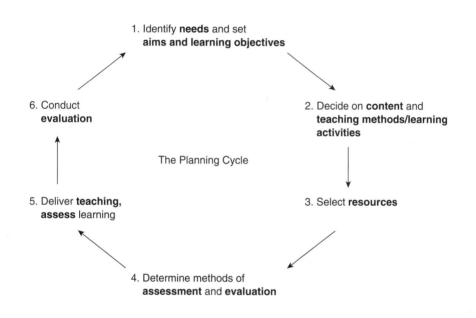

Aims and objectives

After considering the needs of learners, planning starts with aims; but what is meant by the term 'aim' and how does it differ from a learning objective?

We need to have some overall sense of purpose or direction before we can think about the precise nature of the learning that is to take place. We need to consider in broad terms what we, *as teachers*, are trying to achieve. This is how we arrive at the aims of our sessions.

Aims then relate to an overall view of sessions or programmes and help us to answer questions like:

- What is the general purpose of this session or programme?
- Why am I delivering this teaching?
- Why is it worth me including this content in the session or programme?

If you were to ask us why we produced this book, our reply would be 'Because it will be useful to teachers'. You might then probe further, 'Why will it be useful to teachers?' Our response this time would be 'It will provide a broad introduction to the theory and the practical side of teaching', or perhaps 'It will support professionals wanting to gain a teaching qualification'. This would be our **aim**. As you can see, this statement or aim provides a compass setting, so that we have a general idea of the direction in which we wish to travel.

Sometimes it helps to ask additional questions such as:

- 'Why is this teaching worthwhile?'

or

- 'What am I trying to achieve?'

and keep asking, until the answer really expresses, in a concise statement, what you, as the teacher, want to achieve.

Consider the examples in the following illustration.

It can therefore be seen that:

> *An aim is a statement of what the teacher intends the general purpose and direction of the teaching programme should be.*

Activity 5.4

Think now about a programme with which you are involved, or plan to be involved, or maybe a session you are to teach. What do you consider you want to achieve? How does this translate into an aim?

Clear aims are vital to give purpose and direction to planning, but are not specific enough to give details of the actual route. At a more specific level we will now need to think about learning objectives.

We consider a learning objective to be '*a statement that defines the learning that is going to take place*'. The more specific we can be about this learning, the more effective our planning will be. The box at the beginning of each chapter in this book lists the learning objectives for that chapter; it tells you what you will be learning. This is the first important characteristic of a learning objective. It describes the change that learning will bring about; what it is the learner will be able to do that they may not have been able to do before. Consider two of the learning objectives for this chapter:

- Define and distinguish between aims and learning objectives
- Write clear aims and learning objectives for teaching sessions.

We hope you will agree they both describe what you will be learning as part of this chapter, identifying what you will be able to do that you could not do before (assuming that this chapter contains new material or a new way of thinking about things).

Does each of the learning objectives above, however, suggest the same sorts of change? To help you decide, look at the learning objectives listed below, selected from various teaching courses.

At the end of this teaching session each learner will be able to:

1 State three factors influencing radio reception in hilly areas
2 Plant out seedlings
3 Ride a bicycle safely in a straight line for a distance of 100 metres
4 List 10 countries which are currently members of the United Nation
5 State the prime numbers between 0 and 100 in ascending order
6 Construct a T joint from two pieces of wood.

Activity 5.5

How do learning objectives 1, 4 and 5 differ from 2, 3 and 6?

The answers you gave should indicate that learning objectives 1, 4 and 5 are concerned with acquiring knowledge, whereas learning objectives 2, 3 and 6 are to do with acquiring a skill.

Some learning objectives, then, will identify the learning that is to take place in terms of what we now *know* that we did not know before. Other learning objectives do so in terms of what we can now *do* that we could not do before. Sometimes, however, the type of change you aim to bring about in your learners may be less to do with actual knowledge or skills than to do with the *value* they place on these. Your learning objective would then concern attitudes.

Learning objectives therefore fall into three different categories or 'domains'. These are:

1   Knowledge (also referred to as 'cognitive')
2   Skills (also referred to as 'psychomotor')
3   Attitudes (also referred to as 'affective').

Here are two more learning objectives:

1   At the end of the session each learner will be able to list the five characteristics of a well-written learning objective.
2   At the end of the session each learner will know the letters of the Greek alphabet.

Activity 5.6

If you were expert in both these subjects, which of these learning objectives would you find the easier to plan part of a session around?

What problem does the other learning objective pose for you?

You will probably agree that learning objective 1 is the most useful because it describes exactly the outcome we want, whereas learning objective 2 is too vague and ambiguous. After all, what does 'know' the Greek alphabet mean? Does it mean that the learner should be able to:

• Identify all the letters of the Greek alphabet?
• Write all the letters?
• Recall all the letters?
• Recite all the letters?
• Recite all the letters in the correct order?

In each case we are specifying different learning. From our original learning objective, 'know the Greek alphabet', any of these interpretations is acceptable, which makes the outcome uncertain. Learning objectives, then, must be written in a specific manner leading to a common interpretation.

Our other problem with the learning objective 'know the Greek alphabet' is that we will be uncertain whether it has been achieved. If we are not sure exactly what learning is to take place, how can we test it? This is the problem with 'knowing'. It is a process that takes place in learners' heads. We cannot see or hear what goes on inside heads so we need to express the learning in such a way that learners can demonstrate whether or not it has taken place; the evidence of learning lies in the actions learners now perform that they could not perform before learning took place. The second characteristic of learning objectives, then, is that they should be written in such a manner as to be measurable and this is achieved by use of an 'action verb'.

Activity 5.7

In the table below, pick out the examples of good action verbs for writing learning objectives.

For solution, see end of chapter.

define	select	understand	list
realise the significance of	measure	have a good grasp of	justify
really know	construct	label	be aware of
solve	be familiar with	demonstrate	distinguish between
describe	recall	explain	know
think	perform	appreciate	state
prepare	give reasons	report	be acquainted with

A useful word to help you remember the characteristics of a well-written learning objective is **SMART**. The letters of this mnemonic (memory aid) stand for:

Specific	The learning objective should describe the desired learning **exactly**, stating clearly what the learner will be able to do as a result of your teaching. To achieve this, care should be taken in choosing the appropriate action verb. The action verb is the word that comes immediately after *'will be able to ...'*.
Measurable	What the learner will be able to do should be observable. It should result in some form of action that allows you to satisfy yourself that learning has indeed taken place. This may be through listing, naming, explaining, recognising, demonstrating, performing or a number of other different ways in which the learners will show you they *'are able to ...'*.
Achievable	Regardless of how well your learning objective is written – it may be a model of clarity and clearly measurable – it is only of practical use if it is within the capabilities of the intended learners and sufficiently challenging. Learning objectives must be written with the learners in mind, which is why it is important to find out as much as you can about your learners prior to planning. After all it is they who *'will be able to ...'*.
Relevant	What is the point of this learning described by your learning objective? If the learners cannot see why it is important or how it will help them, then they may ask themselves why they should bother *'to be able to ...'*.
Time bound	How long will it take to achieve this learning objective? It may take one session, a week or a lifetime of trying. Learners should be made aware of how long it will be before they can be reasonably expected *'to be able to ...'*.

Learning objectives therefore allow us to:

- Identify clearly the learning that is to take place
- Make appropriate choices of methods and resources
- Select assessment strategies.

Whichever type of objective you will be writing – knowledge, skill or attitude – you will need to ensure these are SMART.

Choosing appropriate methods

We can view teaching methods or learning activities in much the same way as a carpenter, a plumber or an electrician considers the tools in their toolbox. There will be a variety of tools to allow all sorts of tasks to be tackled. The most appropriate tools are selected after the task has been seen and before work commences. Similarly, as teachers, we have a range of methods and activities at our disposal and our skill lies in choosing the most appropriate method for the circumstances in which we find ourselves and then using that method effectively.

The factors that influence our choice of activity/method fall into three categories:

1 The learning that is to take place – the objectives
2 Those who will undertake the learning – the learners
3 The conditions in which the learning will take place – the reality factor.

The objectives

It is evident that we would *not* use particular teaching methods for some objectives. We would not, for instance, be wise to use the lecture method if we want learners to develop a skill, such as tying a knot to secure a boat to a post. Role play would be equally inappropriate to explain the workings of a car engine. It would be difficult to hold a discussion on something strictly factual, like the calculation of the area of a building. It is relatively easy to identify methods we would *not* use, but where do we start in deciding what methods we *do* use? It is apparent that the methods we associate with different subject specialisms stem from the type of learning or learning objectives associated with that subject.

There is some agreement at a basic level that certain activities are more appropriate for certain objectives. These are summarised below:

* Teaching methods appropriate to **knowledge** objectives include: lectures, brain-storming, games, projects, and question and answer
* Methods that support the acquisition of **skills** include: demonstration, practical exercises and simulation
* Methods appropriate for **attitude** objectives include: discussion, games, role play and tutorials.

Use the information from the lists above in the next activity.

Activity 5.8

Select an appropriate teaching method from the list above to achieve the following learning objectives:

Learning objectives

At the end of the teaching session each learner will be able to:

1   State three factors influencing flooding of the River Thames
2   Perform a forward somersault from a standing position
3   Ride a bicycle safely in a straight line for a distance of 100 metres
4   List four countries that became members of the European Community in 2007
5   Recognise the need for protective footwear on a construction site
6   Give four reasons for the increase in obesity in the UK
7   Recognise the importance of teamwork
8   Evaluate the pros and cons of developing renewable energy
9   Lead a walking bus to school
10 List the prime numbers between 0 and 100 in ascending order.

Having made these links, you will appreciate that a key consideration in choosing an appropriate method is the objective that is to be achieved and whether it relates to knowledge, skills or attitudes.

Chapter 8 is concerned with thinking about the teaching of your subject specialism and the knowledge, skills and attitudes that learners need to acquire.

The learners

There are, however, further considerations to be made before arriving at a final decision; whilst the method we choose may fit the objective, it *may not* suit the learner or learners who will be achieving this objective. In Chapter 6 we look at the characteristics of learners that may also have a bearing on our choice of teaching method. Ultimately our choice of method must be one that accommodates both the objective and the learners. Whilst the lecture, for instance, may be an appropriate method for a knowledge objective, we would not use it with a lively group with short attention spans. Instead, we may well opt for a game, which would still be appropriate in achieving the objective but would also engage this particular group of learners.

The reality factor

Our third factor, reality, includes practical considerations such as:

- The time available
- The time of day or year
- The size of the group
- The space in which we will teach them
- The resources that are available to us
- How confident we are in the use of a particular method or resource.

Thinking about these three factors – our objectives, our learners and our context – will help us to make the best choice of methods and ensure that we provide our learners with appropriate learning opportunities.

Chapter summary

The main points covered in this chapter are:

- ✓ Planning a session will make our delivery more effective and save effort next time.
- ✓ Learners should be the first consideration in planning a session.
- ✓ Aims describe the teacher's general purpose.
- ✓ Objectives define the learning that an individual will achieve.
- ✓ Objectives relate to knowledge, skill or attitude and should be SMART – specific, measurable, achievable, relevant and time bound.
- ✓ To choose an appropriate method we need to consider the objective, the learner and the 'reality factor'.

Solution to Activity 5.7

In the table below, the good action verbs for writing learning objectives are shown in **bold**.

define	**select**	understand	**list**
realise the significance of	**measure**	have a good grasp of	**justify**
really know	**construct**	label	be aware of
solve	be familiar with	**demonstrate**	distinguish between
describe	recall	**explain**	know
think	perform	appreciate	**state**
prepare	**give reasons**	report	be acquainted with

 Further reading

Fairclough, M. (2008) *Supporting Learners in the Lifelong Learning Sector*. Maidenhead: McGraw-Hill, Open University Press.
Chapter 7 discusses the differences between aims and objectives and takes a wider look at the planning process in general.

Petty, G. (2009) *Teaching Today* (4th edn). Cheltenham: Nelson Thornes.
Chapter 37 'Aims and Objectives' contains a full discussion of the topic and distinguishes between different types of objectives.

Kerry, T. (1999) *Effective Learning Objectives, Task Setting and Differentiation*. London: Hodder and Stoughton.
A little bit dated, but an easy to read book which covers all of the areas highlighted in the title and illustrates the relationship between learning objectives and methods, assessment and evaluation.

Useful websites

Writing learning objectives and suggested action verbs

www.tss.uoguelph.ca/resources/idres/learningobjectives1.pdf

More action verbs

http://www.wisha.org/CE/Writing%20Learning%20Outcomes%20and%20Assessment%20of.pdf

pink Done feedback

Green for m—

Summary

6

Planning for inclusive learning

Chapter overview

When you have worked through this chapter on planning for inclusive learning you will be able to:

- Recognise the importance of initial assessment
- Identify individual differences and ways in which each may impact on learning
- Promote inclusion
- Select appropriate differentiation strategies
- Define equality and diversity
- Develop equality and diversity guidelines for your own teaching context

This chapter looks at issues of diversity, inclusion, differentiation and equality. Before you begin to work your way through it, reflect upon what these different terms mean.

 Activity 6.1

Define the following terms in your own words:

1 Diversity
2 Inclusion
3 Differentiation
4 Equality

You may want to revisit these definitions as you reach appropriate parts of the chapter. Before focusing on these interrelated issues we need to consider the individual nature of learners in the lifelong learning sector.

Initial assessment of learners

In Chapter 5 on planning, we found out how to write learning objectives in a way that ensures they will be both specific and measurable. An indication of the time in which we would expect the objective to be achieved was given by prefacing each action by the phrase 'by the end of the session each learner will be able to ...'. This covers S, M and T in the 'SMART' mnemonic (memory aid). But how do we make our objectives A (achievable, yet challenging) and R (relevant)?

Achievable and Relevant refer to learners. No matter how technically well written an objective, it is of little practical use if it does not take into account the nature and characteristics of the learners who are to achieve it. Learners in the lifelong learning sector come with a range of previous experiences and a wide range of different backgrounds; we can be certain that each group of learners we come across will possess different characteristics from another group. Perhaps more importantly, the individuals within the group will each be different, as will be their needs and talents.

Recognition of individual differences and needs starts from the moment that learners apply for courses. It is usual to organise an initial interview to make sure that the course applied for matches the learner's aspirations and capabilities. The most effective way we can ensure success is to make sure that learners' individual starting points have been taken into account and that they are on the appropriate course in the first place.

This is the first function of initial assessment. As such, it begins with an examination of the qualifications that learners already hold. These will provide an indication of the level of skills or knowledge already achieved and allow some prediction to be made as to the likelihood of success if the learner is accepted onto the course. A judgement can also be made as to the level of course – foundation, intermediate, advanced – that is best for the particular learner.

Learners may have the appropriate prior learning and have identified a course of the appropriate level, but is the choice of course compatible with their needs, aspirations, interests and career goals? It may be that a purely academic course has been selected when a more vocational choice would better meet their needs. So their choice needs to be discussed at an informal interview where all the possibilities can be examined to make sure that the final choice of course is both appropriate and well informed.

Having successfully placed learners on a course that is appropriate to their abilities and goals, the next function of initial assessment is to identify any kind of additional support that learners may need in order to successfully complete their chosen course of study. Learners may well have different levels of reading, writing, numeracy, language and ICT skills, all of which are crucial in any course that is undertaken, regardless of subject or level. Some adult learners may have attained Maths and English qualifications many years ago. It is likely that such qualifications may no longer give an accurate indication of levels of performance, perhaps due to lack of practice, or the nature of the skills required may have changed in the intervening years.

Diagnostic tests are normally undertaken by all learners in FE to ascertain their competence in these 'functional' skills and identify the possible need for additional support. Learning difficulties, such as dyslexia, can also be identified at this stage. Again, appropriate arrangements can be made for the additional support learners will require in order to cope with the demands of their chosen course. The second function of initial assessment, therefore, is to remove barriers to learning by identifying these at the beginning of the learner's course and to put into place the necessary arrangements to successfully manage them. The process can be taken further by identifying learning styles, making learners aware of their own approaches to learning and introducing them to strategies suited to their own preferences as well as enabling them to deal with situations that favour other approaches.

Most institutions within the lifelong learning sector will have specialists who carry out diagnostic testing, but the results of initial assessments should be made available to teachers and should inform Individual Learning Plans.

Individual differences

It is important to recognise the differences in the learners we teach, as these may influence how we interact with them. To act professionally as teachers we will want to ensure that we behave in ways that are acceptable to all our learners, taking into account factors such as race, gender, age, previous experience or background.

Consider the learners with whom you have had contact so far, or alternatively groups of learners of which you have been a part.

Activity 6.2

What individual differences have you noticed in learners you have met?

The differences you have noted all have implications for the way in which we teach, as each will affect that individual's learning and how we as teachers view that individual. We would not, however, want these differences to lower the expectations we have of any of our learners. Such expectations can, sometimes unwittingly, be transmitted in what we say and how we behave, and this can negatively affect the learning environment we provide for our learners.

Some of the typical individual differences you might encounter are listed below. Each of these may have its own particular effect on teaching and learning:

Age	Physical disability	Mental health issues
Cultural differences	Motivation	Religion
Ethnicity	Attention span	Previous experience
Gender	Personality	Aptitude
Sexual orientation	Learning difficulty	Learning styles

Activity 6.3

Pick *two* of the items you noted in Activity 6.2.

How may each of these two characteristics affect learning?

How might you take this into account when teaching that individual?

As an example, consider the different ways in which we prefer to take in information. When we learn, some of us prefer to take in information through words (either written or spoken), others prefer visual means (pictures, diagrams), whilst others like to engage directly with the information and learn through 'doing'. Although most learners will be able to use several techniques, some will experience difficulties and frustrations when engaging in techniques that do not match their preferred style.

Suppose you get a new computer. You might take the different parts out of the box and try to assemble them, working out which bits connect together, and get the computer to work straight away just by looking at all the different parts and trying to work out which bit connects together. You would do this because your preferred way of accessing information and subsequently learning is through 'doing'. If you could not make it work, however, you might well then unpack the instruction manual and either read it or look at the diagrams it contains for guidance. You might not have looked at the manual first of all, not because you could not understand it, but because your natural preference is to learn through 'doing'. Someone else might start by reading the manual or by looking at the diagrams because that is their preference. One model of categorising individual preferences is 'VAK' – visual, aural, kinaesthetic (for more details, see http://www.brainboxx.co.uk/a3_aspects/pages/VAK.htm).

In any group of learners we meet, it is likely that we will encounter this mix of preferences for taking in information. We could conduct our teaching session by talking and explaining to learners, supporting this by slides with the appropriate definitions and summaries of the main points, on the assumption that most people are capable of taking in some information from words.

An alternative would be to talk and explain to learners, supported by slides with pictures and diagrams of what we are explaining, and then follow this up with some exercises where learners use the information we are trying to put across to them.

In this second approach, we would be trying to ensure that at some stage in the session we cater for each of the different ways of accessing information – we would be trying to ensure that all, and not just some learners, were being accommodated. If we had done an individual analysis of preferred styles we would also be aware at which point the approach might best suit each individual learner.

Activity 6.4

Think of a topic you teach through words only. What else might you do with this topic to suit all learners and the ways in which they prefer to take in information?

Diversity

The above discussion illustrates a number of concepts that are considered to be of great importance within lifelong learning. The range of differences encountered within any group of learners is referred to as diversity. The following definition is given by Clements and Jones (2006: 13):

> *Diversity is defined by 'otherness' or those human qualities that are different from our own and outside the groups to which we belong, yet are present in other individuals or groups. (University of Maryland, 1995)*

Another way of defining diversity is 'Different Individuals Valuing Each other Regardless of Skin, Intellect, Talent or Years' (www.trendenterprises.com). A poster with these words, spelling out Diversity, can be seen on the walls of many lifelong learning establishments to raise awareness of the diversity in the learner population.

Inclusion

Diversity brings richness to the group and provides a wealth of previous experience and contributions that might not otherwise exist. A possible consequence, however, is that some learners will feel excluded, as their particular needs are not being met. If we are to be effective in our teaching, all learners should feel part of and engaged in the particular session. If this is the case, our approach would be said to be demonstrating inclusion.

Inclusion operates at many different levels and in many different contexts. Tomlinson (1996: 26) defined inclusion as 'the greatest degree of match or fit between individual learning requirements and provision'. The major concern of his report was the 'inclusion' of students with learning difficulties and disabilities in mainstream college provision, but from a more general viewpoint we can consider inclusive teaching as teaching that allows *all* learners to potentially benefit and learn from any aspect of a teaching session. Inclusion is both about planning so that all learners are included and also about learners *feeling* included.

Differentiation

The strategies we use to ensure inclusion in the learning environment/teaching context are collectively known as differentiation strategies.

Activity 6.5

What differentiation strategies have you experienced as a learner or used in your teaching sessions?

When introducing material to a whole group, a variety of methods can be used to take account of the different preferred learning styles, attitudes and motivation of individual learners within the group. Presentation methods may differentiate in terms of learners accessing the material, as previously explained, but they are teacher-led and may not sufficiently take account of the different levels of understanding or previous experience learners have within the particular topic.

Activities that encourage learners to use and process the information are much more successful in allowing individuals to engage in learning at an appropriate level. Generally, the more open an activity and the more you give control to learners, the more the level is self-regulated and learning occurs at a manageable but challenging level for each individual. It can be argued that, given the opportunity, learners themselves manage differentiation more effectively than teachers. Open activities are not always possible, however, and as teachers we can use a number of different strategies to achieve a more differentiated and inclusive approach to teaching and learning.

Differentiation can be achieved in a number of different ways:

1 Within any group that you teach, there may well be individual learners with specific needs relating to some form of learning difficulty or disability. Institutions have different methods of requesting that learners self-disclose any learning difficulty or disability on enrolment, and will then normally provide support, such as hearing loops or signers for hearing-impaired learners, adaptive software for visually impaired learners and scribes/software for those learners with communication difficulties such as severe dyslexia. Organisations such as AbilityNet can supply enabling resources. These can be supplemented by simpler 'teacher-initiated' measures such as a consideration of seating positions, clear enunciation, enlarged print on handouts and other written material, use of coloured paper (different colours suit individual learners) and appropriate fonts (Comic Sans font on blue paper, for instance, may be helpful for some learners with dyslexia).

   Despite your best efforts you may not be fully aware of all those within your group who have a learning difficulty or disability, as this is, to a large extent, dependent on learner self-disclosure. This can make it difficult for the teacher to identify and respond with the appropriate support. Irregular attendance, for example, can be caused by mental health issues which learners may choose not to disclose. If you, as a teacher, are aware of the issue it is easier to propose adjustments.

2 If we set a single learning objective for a whole group, it is likely that it will not be appropriate for all learners, as, whilst it may be achievable by the majority, it may be too easy or too difficult for others, due to the diversity of the group. At this stage it is useful to look at the classic work of Benjamin Bloom (1956), who, in his *Taxonomy of Educational Objectives*, introduced the idea of different levels of performance. If a learning objective is concerned with knowledge, for instance, Bloom identified six different levels of performance:

   • Knowledge – being able to recall or recognise the material to be learned
   • Comprehension – understanding the learned material
   • Application – putting the learned material to use
   • Analysis – breaking down the learned material and drawing conclusions
   • Synthesis – using the learned material to form new ideas
   • Evaluation – using the learned material to make judgements, present and defend opinions.

If we apply this to a physics lesson on electricity, we could write the following learning objective:

   • By the end of this session each learner will be able to describe the differences between a series and a parallel circuit.

This is an objective that looks for Comprehension and may be appropriate for most, but if applied to a diverse group may be too difficult for some and too easy for others. One possibility in this situation is to have supplementary objectives, one of which might be at a lower level of Bloom's Taxonomy, looking only for Knowledge:

- By the end of this session each learner will be able to identify examples of series and parallel circuits.

and one of which might address the next higher level, of Application:

- By the end of this session each learner will be able to decide whether a series or parallel circuit is appropriate for a given situation.

Although the group as a whole might be covering the same topic, learning is personalised so that different outcomes can be achieved within it, ensuring all learners succeed and are challenged. We can achieve this through group work using graduated tasks or worksheets, or by supplying extra resource material as required. So, you can achieve differentiation through setting different levels of learning objective.

3   We may decide to have learners working either individually or in groups on the same learning outcome. Some may finish earlier than others and some may find difficulty in completing the task. Our problem is to keep those who have finished early occupied and stretched whilst having time to give extra assistance to those who need it. To give the early finishers 'more of the same' is not the best option. Instead, you can have an 'extension task' ready and you simply tell learners what this is at the appropriate time, or have it available in written form. An extension task covers the same content but takes learners up to the next level of Bloom's Taxonomy. If the original learning objective was at the 'Knowledge' level, the extension task would take learners up to the 'Comprehension' level, and so on. You can then take feedback at the end of the activity, which incorporates the extension task as well as the original learning objective.

4   When setting up group work, we should think carefully about the composition of the group. If, for instance, we have a fairly diverse group as a whole, how can we ensure that when we break this into smaller groups, we are creating a differentiated environment? One possibility is to group learners by expertise. The more expert groups can get on with the task, giving us the time to spend with those learners who are in most need of it. On the other hand, we can form groups with a spread of expertise, with the more expert members of the group providing support to those who need to develop further. We can then be more responsive to the moment in terms of allocating our attention. There may well be other possibilities that provide better differentiation, depending upon the needs of the particular group and the individual learners within it, but the point is that the setting up of group work provides an opportunity to ensure a differentiated approach. If you place learners in different groups for different tasks they can work with a wider range of people and increase their feeling of inclusion – although this will only happen if a positive social environment is created within which learners feel confident to learn (see Chapter 2).

5   Directed questioning can also provide a route to a differentiated approach. Simpler questions would be directed to less confident learners and more challenging supplementary questions could be directed towards learners who need to be stretched.

6   The most personalised approach to meeting individual needs within a diverse group is to set individual objectives and tasks on an Individual Learning Plan. This can be achieved within a workshop or project setting where learners work independently from each other. When you reach Chapter 13 on planning, you will see that the planning format for workshops encourages the setting of individual objectives and monitoring progress at an individual level. Potentially, learners can become involved in the setting of their own objectives.

The best way to examine your practice with respect to differentiation is to look back after teaching a session and analyse what you did and what the learners thought of it (Chapter 14 on evaluation provides some useful guidance on self-evaluation). If you are at all sensitive to the needs of your learners, you will undoubtedly find that although you may not have planned it, or even realised that you were doing it, you will have differentiated in some manner and have involved learners in this process. Recognising this is the first step to becoming more aware of the issue and beginning to differentiate in a more systematic and deliberate manner. Another possibility is to observe another teacher and spot any strategies they may have used, or, alternatively, reflect back on your own learning and identify times when you felt truly 'included'.

 Activity 6.6

Identify at least two new differentiation strategies you could use in your teaching.

Equality

Inclusion is very much related to issues of equality. Within the context of lifelong learning, equality is considered to encompass:

- An expectation of fair treatment
- An opportunity to participate on equal terms.

 Activity 6.7

Does equality mean we should treat all learners in the same manner or differently? Why and what examples can you provide?

An expectation of fair treatment requires us as teachers to be non-judgemental and accept that people see the world differently and that these world-views have equal validity. We need not agree with all opinions that are expressed, and may well wish to challenge and debate some of them, but this does not mean that we do not recognise the right of our learners to hold different opinions. This aspect of equality and diversity requires us to value and treat all learners fairly, in the same consistent manner, 'without fear or favour', with dignity and respect. We would doubtless all claim to do this, but it is inevitable that our views of learners will be subject to some bias – we are only human after all.

The section on reliability in assessment (see Chapter 10) illustrates how difficult it is to adopt a totally non-judgemental, accepting position towards all learners, whether we are aware of it or not. Other issues, such as stereotyping of learners and presenting stereotypical views to learners also come into play here. We need to be aware of our own prejudices and how these shape our behaviour, especially as, in our role as teachers, our behaviour can shape the attitudes and behaviours of our learners.

The second aspect of equality acknowledges that we recognise learners do not all start from the same point, and we need to take account of this in our planning. The institution that you work in will have a policy related to Equality and Diversity to address such matters.

Examples of institutional support include crèche facilities, provided for learners with need for childcare; and bursaries available for those for whom finance represents a barrier to access. At the level of individual teaching sessions, equality of access can be a key issue. Ramps and lifts may be provided for learners with a physical disability or classes timetabled in ground floor accommodation to ensure that 'reasonable adjustments' are made. Within a teaching session, similar barriers may exist – access to resources, access to the teacher's time and support, for instance – and we need to be aware of these.

Activity 6.8

Devise Equality and Diversity guidelines for the sessions that you teach.

Initial assessment may have identified those who require additional support with areas such as literacy or numeracy. Most institutions will provide additional learning support, either on an individual or group basis, as well as a number of other kinds of student support designed to allow all learners to compete on equal terms.

It can be seen that issues of diversity, equality and inclusion permeate the teaching and learning process and operate at all different levels – individual, group, institution and society. These issues will need to be kept in mind as you read Chapter 7 on learning individually and in groups and Chapter 8 on methods for teaching different subject specialisms.

Chapter summary

- ✓ Initial assessment establishes that learners are on the most appropriate courses to meet their individual needs, and, where necessary, suitable arrangements for additional support can be made quickly and effectively.
- ✓ Learners in the lifelong learning sector exhibit a wide range of individual differences which can influence the ways in which learning takes place. Diversity is the term used to describe this range of differences.
- ✓ Inclusion is the process whereby *all* learners are made to feel part of the learning process.
- ✓ Differentiation is the term used to describe the strategies used to achieve an inclusive approach.
- ✓ Differentiation can be achieved in a number of ways, such as setting learning objectives at different levels and using extension tasks.
- ✓ Equality involves the fair and consistent treatment of learners, whilst ensuring equality of opportunity in participating in learning.
- ✓ All of the above issues operate at national, institutional, group and individual levels.

→ References

Bloom, B. (1956) *Taxonomy of Educational Objectives: Handbook 1*. New York: Longman.

Clements, P. and Jones, J. (2006) *The Diversity Training Handbook* (2nd edn). London: Kogan Page [quoting University of Maryland (1995) www.inform.umd.edu].

Tomlinson, J. (1996) *Report of the Further Education Funding Council Learning Difficulties and/or Disabilities Committee*. Coventry: FEFC.

Further reading

Kerry, T. (1999) *Effective Learning Objectives, Task Setting and Differentiation*. London: Hodder and Stoughton.
An easy-to-read book with a variety of strategies that can be used for differentiation.

Powell, S. and Tummons, J. (2011) *Inclusive Practice in the Lifelong Learning Sector*. Exeter: Learning Matters.
A good general text on issues surrounding inclusion. In Chapter 6, a case study approach is taken to look at 'inclusive learning and teaching practices'.

Race, P. (2010) *Making Learning Happen: A Guide for Post Compulsory Education* (2nd edn). London: Sage Publications.
Chapter 8 discusses the changing nature of learners in post-compulsory education and gives detail on specific special needs.

Petty, G. (2009) *Teaching Today – A Practical Guide* (4th edn). Cheltenham: Nelson Thornes. A useful overview of several different aspects of diversity, with checklists against which to compare your own practice. For an interesting account of the relationship between stereotyping and equality, see Chapter 7.

Useful websites

Link to the Equality Act 2010

http://www.homeoffice.gov.uk/equalities/equality-act/

Links to different examples of good practice in differentiation

http://archive.excellencegateway.org.uk/page.aspx?o=131299

Suggested differentiation strategies

http://members.shaw.ca/priscillatheroux/differentiatingstrategies.html

British Dyslexia Association

http://www.bdadyslexia.org.uk/

7

Learning individually and in groups

Chapter overview

When you have worked through this chapter on learning individually and in groups you will be able to:

- Define 'group' and what characterises a 'learning group'
- State the potential benefits of being part of a learning group
- Outline different choices of group activity
- Identify the stages of group formation and how these might be managed
- Plan, set up and conclude small group work
- Select an appropriate method of taking feedback from group work
- Identify instances where one-to-one contact between teacher and learner leads to the most effective learning
- List the benefits of one-to-one contact
- Describe the functions of Individual Learning Plans (ILPs) and learning contracts

Working with groups

In the last chapter we focused on how best we can plan inclusively so that all our individual learners can respond effectively to the learning context. As we manage the learning environment we need to consider in what circumstances an individual will learn most effectively – on their own, in small groups or in a whole group. In this chapter we will focus on learning in groups.

What is a group?

We use the word 'group' widely in everyday speech; but what does this term mean? Is it more than just a number of people in the same space at the same time?

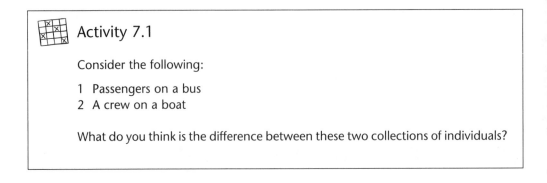

Activity 7.1

Consider the following:

1 Passengers on a bus
2 A crew on a boat

What do you think is the difference between these two collections of individuals?

As you will have deduced from this activity, if people gather in the same space at the same time it does not necessarily mean they will function as a group.

Activity 7.2

Can you name three groups to which you belong?

What do these groups have in common?

The questions above will have prompted you to reflect on what makes a collection of individuals a group.

Members of groups normally:

- Have some common purpose, goal or task that they wish to achieve together
- Interact with each other to achieve this
- Identify with others as belonging to the group
- Recognise and usually conform to norms which relate to what they do and how they do it.

Activity 7.3

Can you think of any benefits to learners if they are part of a group?

You may have noted benefits such as:

- Group members can share and pool a wide range of knowledge, experience and learning from others
- The group can often achieve more than individuals achieve on their own
- Individual group members can help each other, providing mutual support
- The diversity in a group can result in a differentiated learning environment
- Working in a group provides an opportunity for individuals to develop additional skills, such as communication or problem solving
- Group work adds variety to the teaching context and can refocus learner attention.

You may conclude from this that, if learners become part of a learning group, it can enhance their learning, but fully functioning learning groups do not form instantly.

Moving towards a performing group

A group of individuals become a learning group gradually, in a series of developmental stages, as you will have noted when we discussed 'breaking the ice' in Chapter 2. The model of group development provided by Tuckman (1965) is the best known and has four stages: forming, storming, norming and performing.

1 Forming – Coming together of the members of the potential group; members try to identify how the group will operate and their place in it.
2 Storming – Members jostle for position and a 'pecking order' begins to emerge.
3 Norming – 'Norms', or expectations of behaviour, from those in the group, begin to emerge. The group develops some cohesion.
4 Performing – The group begins to function as a learning unit; members work together to achieve their common goals, learners provide mutual support for each other and begin to derive benefits from being a group member.

It helps if groups reach the performing stage as quickly as possible. We wish, therefore, to establish a group learning environment in which individuals feel valued, supported, confident and able to maximise their learning.

 Activity 7.4

How can you encourage groups to reach the performing stage as quickly as possible?

The forming and storming stages of group development are most easily achieved as learners communicate with each other and begin to feel more at ease in each other's company. An obvious start is an icebreaking activity, as discussed in Chapter 2, which 'encourages learners to talk to us, to each other and to the group as a whole'.

Small group activities used in the early stages of a course, in which the composition of the groups is constantly changed, encourage mixing within the group and talking to and getting to know other group members. Reaching agreement on ground rules (Chapter 2) can also speed up the process of establishing group norms.

We can encourage groups to become performing groups by selecting carefully the types of group work that our learners engage in and the way in which we facilitate their group activity.

We will focus here on learning in small groups and focus on strategies more appropriate for the teaching of whole groups in the next chapter.

Different forms of group work

> ### Activity 7.5
>
> What different types of group work have you experienced?

Small group activities can take a variety of different forms. Some of the more common ones are:

Buzz groups
Small groups are set up and given a specific task to complete or an issue to consider in a fairly short time. The different groups may all work on the same task or issue, or different aspects of it, sharing their conclusions in a plenary session at the end of the activity. The name is taken from the buzz of conversation produced around the room when the activity is in full flow.

Brainstorming groups
The groups produce as large a number of creative ideas as possible, within a short time frame, to discuss and evaluate at a later stage. All ideas are acceptable and become common property.

Snowball
The name snowball reflects the way the groups gradually increase in size, like a snowball rolling down a hill. Learners first consider an issue individually and jot down their thoughts. They then form pairs and compare notes, looking for similarities

and differences. The pairs then combine to form groups of four for further discussion, arriving at a conclusion which they can report back in a plenary session. This type of group activity is particularly useful when learners are still fairly new to each other, as it starts off with an individual learner talking just to one other person, having had time to think about what they say, before contributing to the larger group.

Crossover groups

Groups are given a specific topic to discuss. At the end of the allotted period of time the crossover occurs, one member from each group joins together to form new groups. This maximises the exchange of information between group members. In a class of 25 this works well with five learners in each group.

Differentiated groups

A wide ranging topic can be split into different aspects, each of which can be allocated to different groups, contributions being shared in a plenary session at the end. The more challenging and less challenging aspects of the topic can be allocated to different groups depending on their experience or familiarity within this particular area. In this way learners achieve differentiated learning objectives (see Chapter 6).

The circus

Each group completes a set of tasks in a different order. This allows very effective use of limited resources, for example reference material, computers or laboratory equipment. Consideration needs to be given, in advance, to the duration of each task and how to ensure smooth and safe transitions as groups move between activities.

Managing group work

 Activity 7.6

> Think of occasions when you have worked successfully in a small group activity. What made this a good learning experience for you? Think of occasions when you found working in small groups frustrating or unsatisfactory? Why was this?

Hopefully, this activity has caused you to reflect on what we can do as teachers to ensure that working in small groups is effective for learning. You are likely to find that your ideas relate to one of the following four categories: planning; setting up group activity; monitoring groups and maintaining energy; concluding and closing.

Planning

Many of the potential limitations of learners working in small groups can be overcome by thorough planning prior to the commencement of the activity they are to engage in.

If we plan and set up group work well then the outcome is normally more favourable.

Decide on the purpose of the activity

First we need to ensure that group work is the most suitable activity for the objectives that you wish to achieve.

Questions you might want to ask yourself are:

- Has the group adequate underpinning knowledge and experience to achieve the task? (This may have been achieved through a lecture or whole group presentation earlier in the scheme of work.)
- Does the topic lend itself to collaboration?
- Does the topic lend itself to discussion, sharing and reflection on experiences or opinions?
- Is the topic sufficiently complex to sustain a meaningful group discussion?
- Does it involve making judgements or applying general principles to practical situations?
- Is it capable of resolution within the available time and health and safety requirements?
- Can it be completed with only infrequent help from the teacher?

Size and composition of groups

The larger the group the greater the knowledge and experience there is for group members to draw upon and reach a considered outcome. A smaller group, however, is likely to reach a decision more quickly and involve all of its members in some capacity in the group activity.

So, any decision on group size will involve a compromise. Petty (2009: 243) suggests that 'Up to six and many hands make light work; over eight and too many cooks spoil the broth'. Jaques and Salmon (2007: 25) support this view suggesting, 'Most theorists, researchers and practitioners agree that five to seven members is the optimum for leaderless groups'.

Activity 7.7

What do you think needs to be considered when combining particular learners to work together most effectively in a group?

The kinds of factors that might be considered in arriving at a decision include:

- If the prime purpose of the task is social, learners can be randomly allocated to groups or numbered off, the purpose being to achieve social mixing within the group as a whole
- If the purpose is task orientated, the nature of the task may require you to ensure a balance of learners with particular experience or areas of expertise in each group, so that learners can support each other
- If you wish to employ differentiation strategies you may choose to group learners in terms of aptitude for the task in hand. This will enable you to spend more time with any group which encounters more difficulty
- The compatibility of learners also needs to be considered. Are there any combinations of learners which will lead to personality clashes? Are there some learners who are better working apart? Are some friendship groupings likely to become too social and lose focus on the task?

Thinking through these issues in advance leads to more productive group working.

Setting up group work

Introduction

A good introduction ensures that learners have a clear idea of the purpose of the activity, how it is to be carried out and how much time it will take.

This requires you to state the task very clearly and break it down if necessary. This can be achieved by explaining the activity and/or providing written instructions, perhaps on a PowerPoint slide, the whiteboard or a handout, which can be used for future reference. Identifying a definite end product (report back, short presentation, flip chart notes or completion of hand-out) is important as it helps to keep the group focused on the task in hand. An example of what is expected often helps to avoid potential misunderstandings and clarify exactly what is required. It is best not to allow the activity to start until you say so and are sure that everyone understands the task and knows what is expected of them.

Ground rules

Establishing some ground rules for the group work can influence the quality of the outcome. For example, agreeing to value and respond to other group member's contributions, to take collective responsibility for time keeping, or requiring specific group members to take on roles (chair, scribe, reporter) can encourage more effective participation for the duration of the activity.

Monitoring and maintaining energy levels

Monitoring progress is essential to ensure the most effective use of time for learning, but this can be done unobtrusively. Groups will need time to settle before it is worth checking that each group understands the task to be undertaken and is making a positive start. Merely scanning the room every few minutes will give you some clues as to whether learners are engaged and ground rules being observed. You can then circulate and position yourself near enough to each group to note what is happening and, if necessary, briefly intervene to ensure that focus is maintained on the task.

The key to good control of group work is 'withitness', the ability to have 'eyes in the back of your head' and talk to members of one group whilst always being positioned so that you can be alert to the activity of others.

One thing you will be monitoring is the energy level within each group, the amount of buzzing conversation and positive body language. Groups can progress through a task at different rates so pre-prepared extension tasks can be allocated to early finishers to maintain involvement.

Concluding and closing

The monitoring process described above will help us to decide when group work should be concluded. If groups are working well and discussion is productive we may well decide to let the activity continue beyond the time allocated. If, on the other hand, you consider that discussion is flagging and has run its course, it is best to end the task.

It is now important to acknowledge the results of the work that has taken place and reinforce the learning that has taken place. If this is not done, learners may question the point of the activity and be less keen to engage in group work in the future.

Sharing the results of group activity can be achieved in a number of ways, as identified earlier (report back, short presentation, flip chart notes, completion of hand-out), but the role of the teacher at this stage is to clarify, summarise and make some form of record of the conclusions reached.

When taking feedback, if the first group makes a lengthy contribution, it can leave subsequent groups with very little or nothing to report back. It is therefore important to engage all of the various groups in this activity, and to consider in advance how to achieve the most learning from this activity. Some suggested approaches are given below.

Feedback	Advantages and limitations
Each group reports back in turn	Every group's contribution can be valued but can be repetitious
Each group adds to the last group's contribution	Makes good use of time but the last group may have nothing left to add
Each group reports back on different aspects	Provides variety but may need additional resource to ensure learners record all the feedback
Each person in the group makes a personal statement of what has been learned, also free to 'pass'	The 'round' gives everyone a chance to feedback but can be time consuming and bitty

We noted earlier that the beginning and ends of sessions are crucial times in classroom management. Timing of the feedback session, which often occurs at the ends of a session, is all important. Unless you allow sufficient time feedback is rushed, summaries and conclusions are omitted and learners are less likely to remember the key learning points.

Working one-to-one

So far in this chapter we have looked at the benefits of learning in small groups and how we as teachers or trainers can best manage this type of activity. It is evident that well organised group work can be beneficial to learners, but sometimes, due to the diverse nature of learners or the demands of the task, the learning and development of individual learners can be more effectively achieved if conducted on a one-to-one basis.

Examples of this include:

- Supporting individual projects or research-based learning
- One-to-one contact in workshop situations when practising or acquiring a skill
- Support at an individual level when a group has very diverse needs such as might be found in a Functional Skills or Learning Support environment
- Tutorial sessions
- Work-based learning visits
- Supporting learners on distance learning programmes, possibly using a virtual learning environment (VLE).

Characteristics of one-to-one

 Activity 7.8

Think back to occasions when you have had one-to-one contact with your teacher/tutor, or instances when you have met with learners on a one-to-one basis. What do you see as the particular advantages of working this way?

You may have found that informal one-to-one contact during large or small group sessions has helped clarify or extend understanding of the topic under discussion. Whilst learning a skill, one-to-one contact may have identified correct and inadequate performance and led to suggestions as to what needed to be done to bring about improvement. Individual tutorials may have provided the motivation to keep on top of workloads and addressed any barriers to achieving this. Discussions of individual progress will have helped identify strengths and how to build on these, and will have provided an opportunity to identify individual needs and ways of meeting these.

Sometimes an individual approach is used with a specific aim in mind, such as in coaching where the coach reviews existing skills and devises strategies to refine and improve them. Mentoring involves general development through sharing and learning from the experiences of a more experienced colleague.

What appears to be common in all of these examples is:

- Learners can work at their own pace
- Learning is viewed from the perspective of the learner
- Individual issues or barriers to learning are addressed
- Learners can influence the direction their learning will take
- Individual attention can build confidence.

From a teacher's perspective, one-to-one contact offers the opportunity to get to know our individual learners better, their particular characteristics and preferred ways of learning and to establish a different type of relationship. In turn, this allows learners to use the teacher much more as a resource and exert more control over the pace and direction of the session. Overall, learners' needs can be more fully addressed and teaching approaches can be tailored to the individual case.

The situation will determine precisely how one-to-one activity is carried out, but the actual methods used will in many instances be similar to those used in the teaching of groups – explaining, questioning, problem-solving exercises, demonstration, practical activity, providing feedback – but are carried out in a more informal and facilitative manner. Despite this informality, the process of one-to-one teaching requires a structure to be productive, accompanied by some element of formal recording which shows evidence of:

- Identification of individual needs
- Choice of appropriate strategies to address these
- An action plan with appropriate parameters
- Periodic review of progress
- Evidence of successful achievement
- Directions for further development.

Structuring one-to-one learning

You will see in Chapter 13 how session planning can take on an individual nature and involve learners in negotiating their own targets when they are involved in project work or in a workshop situation. Another approach to recording individual development is the Individual Learning Plan (ILP). An example can be found on the Excellence Gateway site (http://archive.excellencegateway.org.uk/page.aspx?o=11259).

Learning contracts are often used with adult learners to fulfil a similar function to the ILP. A learning contract is quite simply an agreement drawn up between a teacher and a learner specifying the learning that is to take place and how it is to be achieved and assessed. An example format is shown below. The learning contract is normally completed either as a joint venture between teacher and learner, or by the individual learner before checking its contents with the teacher.

Learning contract

Course:_____
Name: _____

1. **What are you going to learn**
   (State learning objectives using SMART terminology)

2. **How will you achieve this?**
   (List the strategies you will employ)

3. **What will you need?**
   (Identify any resources you think you will need)

4. **How will you know that you have been successful in your learning?**
   (Describe how you will evidence that learning has taken place)

5. **By what date will you have completed this contract?**
   (Identify a realistic target date for completion)

Signed_____ (Learner)_____ Date: _____
Signed_____ (Tutor)_____ Date: _____

One-to-one teaching is not always conducted in such a deliberate fashion, however, and in most of the teaching we do, group and individual approaches complement each other. Most sessions have some kind of practical or small group elements built into them which also provide the chance to interact informally with learners on a one-to-one basis. We need to make the most of these spontaneous opportunities.

In this chapter we have looked at the benefits of learning in small groups and individually and how we as teachers or trainers can facilitate this. In the next chapter we focus attention on teaching your specialism and the choice of other activities we can select to aid learning.

Chapter summary

- ✓ Well formed groups display the characteristics of: common purpose, interaction, mutual identification and adherence to group norms.
- ✓ Groups come together in a series of stages. Tuckman (1965) names these as forming, storming, norming and performing.
- ✓ Groups can reach the performing stage more quickly through careful management of the group process.
- ✓ Working in small groups can take a number of forms such as buzz groups, brainstorming groups and snowballing.
- ✓ Effective group work has a clearly defined purpose.
- ✓ An initial consideration of group size and composition contributes to the success of group work.
- ✓ The management of group work involves setting up, monitoring and bringing to a conclusion.
- ✓ The taking of group feedback should be an inclusive process.
- ✓ One-to-one contact can be of significant benefit to individual learners.
- ✓ Individual Learning Plans can be used to provide structure to one-to-one contact between teacher and learner.

→ References

Jaques, D. and Salmon, G. (2007) *Learning in Groups: A Handbook for Face-to-face and Online Environments* (4th edn). London: Routledge.

Petty, G. (2009) *Teaching Today: A Practical Guide* (4th edn). Cheltenham: Nelson Thornes.

Tuckman, B. (1965) 'Developmental Sequence in Small Groups', *Psychological Bulletin* 63: 384–99.

Further reading

Johnson, D.W. and Johnson, F.P. (2002) *Joining Together: Group Theory and Group Skills* (8th edn). Needham Heights, MA: Allyn & Bacon.
Contains the answer to any question you may have on groups.

Rogers, A. and Horrocks, N. (2010) *Teaching Adults* (4th edn). Maidenhead: McGraw-Hill Education, Open University Press.

Chapter 8 provides an in-depth but readable account of various aspects of adult groups, including group formation, advantages and disadvantages and the dynamics of different group seating patterns.

Useful websites

Summary of Tuckman's model with additional fifth stage
  http://www.chimaeraconsulting.com/tuckman.htm

Managing group work
  http://www.assetproject.info/learner_methodologies/during/groupwork.htm

Teaching your specialism

Chapter overview

When you have worked through this chapter on teaching your specialism you will be able to:

- **Recognise the importance of the three types of learning objective in all subject specialisms**
- **Maintain attention when teaching theory-based sessions**
- **Ask questions and deal with the responses they receive**
- **Analyse a skill**
- **Carry out an effective demonstration and monitor progress in the acquisition of a skill**
- **Recognise the components of an attitude**
- **Plan and manage an effective discussion**
- **Plan and manage role play**

This chapter encourages you to look at the teaching and learning strategies that might be used in the teaching of your particular specialism. Chapter 5 suggested that choices of strategy be made not on the basis of subject but after a consideration of the type of objective to be achieved, the nature of the learners who are to achieve it and the various relevant practical considerations. Certain subjects do, however, seem to be taught in a particular manner. Those which are regarded as being more theoretical in nature, such as AS, A level or HE subjects, tend to be taught using a mixture of explanation, supported by visual aids and questioning. Other subjects falling within the general headings of hair and beauty, construction and engineering are considered to have a practical bias and tend to rely largely on demonstration and practice. Other subjects such as counselling are more attitudinal in nature and tend to use strategies such as discussion and small group work. In reality, however, the issue is not as clear cut, as the teaching of *any* subject involves some aspects of theory, practice and the establishing of appropriate attitudes.

It is the exact nature of the subject and qualification which determines the relative importance and degree to which each is represented.

Consider the following:

Functional Skills – Involves the acquisition of literacy and numeracy skills and knowledge, but the biggest barrier to success often lies in learners' negative attitudes towards the subject or themselves.

Bricklaying – Whilst the ultimate goal is the skill of laying bricks, accompanied by a positive attitude towards standards of workmanship and matters of health and safety, this is underpinned by a substantial body of knowledge or theory.

Maths – This can be a highly theoretical subject which demands attention to detail, but cannot be applied without extensive practice of the skills involved.

Nursing – Whilst medical knowledge and skills are of paramount importance, attitudes towards patients play a large part in successful nursing.

Hairdressing – Application of a skill and appropriate attitudes towards clients are the outward signs of the successful learner in this subject but this cannot be achieved without learning the underlying theory.

Accountancy – A knowledge of debit and credit, aligned with attitudes to accuracy and integrity, is required prior to 'balancing the books'.

The headings of 'theory', 'skill' and 'attitudinally' based subjects are used in this chapter to provide a structure, not particularly as a distinction between subject areas. Although you will find some sections more directly applicable to your own particular specialist area, you should find something of relevance in all sections.

Theory-based subjects

Traditionally, the lecture has formed the standard approach to delivering knowledge or theory to learners. This may still be the case in some areas of Higher Education, but generally we take a more informal approach with less of a focus on delivering information and a greater concern for providing an effective and more satisfying learning experience. The term 'lecture' is now less frequently used, and although some form of 'explanation' or 'teacher talk' is still the predominant approach used in the teaching of theory, it is characterised by:

* Shorter periods of teacher talk or explanation
* An increase in two-way rather than one-way communication
* Activities to use and consolidate what has been learned.

This stems from a number of factors.

Active and passive learning

Passive learning involves learners only in receiving information, either verbally or visually. Active learning means that as well as receiving information, learners also actively engage with and use the material to be learned. The significance of the two categories can be seen in the diagram below, an adaptation of Dale's (1969) Cone of Learning. This suggests that we remember far less of what is presented to us when passive rather than active methods are used.

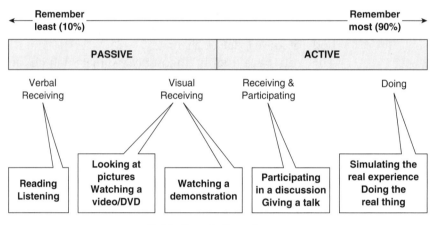

Dale's Cone in linear form

In a typical traditional lecture situation, learners are often only passively involved in their learning – listening to the teacher, looking at the occasional overhead or PowerPoint slide and taking notes. So, although a lot of material is covered, how much of it is understood and subsequently remembered? According to Dale, the amount remembered would be increased considerably if we were to mix teacher talk with activities which involve active learning.

Active learning involves 'doing' and thinking about the information presented either individually or along with other learners. Group activities discussed in the last chapter, like brainstorming or working together in pairs or small 'buzz' groups in which short tasks are completed, responding to brief case studies or problem-solving exercises, creating diagrams, charts or posters, all fall into this category. The common factor in these activities is that they involve learners in thinking about and using the information they have been given.

 Activity 8.1

Think back to the last bit of theory that you taught. How much time did you spend in 'teacher talk'? Can you identify any activities that you could use which involve active learning?

Attention spans

The curve in the digram below represents the way in which learner attention levels vary with time.

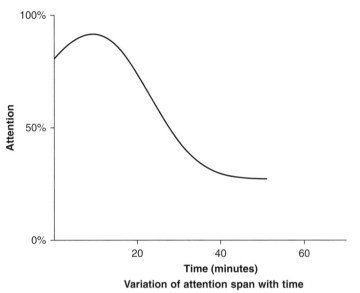

Variation of attention span with time

It tells us that attention levels are high at the beginning of a period of learning, but fall away after a short period of time. During periods of uninterrupted talk by teachers, estimates of high attention levels vary from about 12 to 20 minutes. Generally, active approaches such as those described above, hold attention for a longer period of time than passive approaches and so attention spans can be increased by introducing an interactive element into talks and explanations such as questioning and discussion of answers. This cannot solve the problem completely, however, and so when attention levels begin to drop again we would normally switch to another activity. Each time we change the activity, the curve (and thus higher attention levels) starts again.

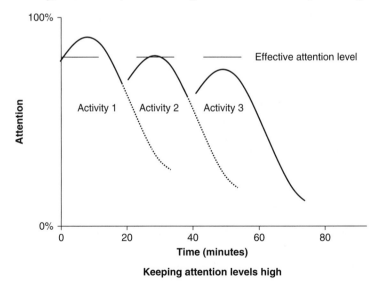

Keeping attention levels high

One of the reasons for short attention spans is to do with the way in which we take in information through the senses. As we will see in Chapter 9, sight is the sense upon which we are most reliant under normal circumstances. When we listen to uninterrupted talk, however, we have to rely solely on hearing. This is not natural and to focus exclusively on the spoken word involves a lot of hard work on our part. We can only maintain this level of effort for a limited period of time.

To relieve the burden on hearing we can use visual aids, which bring the major sense of sight back into play. Visual aids, used appropriately, enhance the delivery of theory by:

- Focusing attention on the important points and emphasising structure
- Creating interest and helping prolong concentration
- Making it easier to understand the material being presented
- Helping learners to remember information
- Giving our ears a rest!

Divided attention

If you are reading a book, can you also watch television at the same time? You may well argue that this is indeed possible, but there would be parts of the TV programme that you would completely miss because, at that time, your attention was focused on your reading. Similarly, your reading would be of a 'stop, start' nature as you periodically turned your attention to the television.

Generally, it is difficult to split or divide attention between two activities, particularly when, as in the above example, they involve the same sense. A similar situation exists when learners make notes during a teaching session, dividing attention between this and listening, to the detriment of both. The necessity for notes will partly depend upon the complexity and familiarity of the material being covered, but, regardless of this, there is a feeling of reassurance in the act of note taking. Whilst we can encourage learners to develop their own methods of effective note taking, such as using abbreviations, bullet points, numbers or perhaps recording notes in the form of questions, we can also contribute more directly to helping with note taking.

We can either supply the notes themselves or provide a framework, such as a gapped handout, within which learners can produce their own notes; this minimises divided attention and helps increase the accuracy of the notes taken. Alternatively, we can make learners aware in advance that we will:

- Avoid unnecessary note taking by highlighting main points visually
- Pause after the main points
- Summarise periodically, giving a few moments to record the point made.

Question and answer

Activity 8.2

What purposes do you think questioning achieves as part of the learning process?

Question and answer can be used to break up teacher talk and encourage participation. Questioning by the teacher can accomplish a variety of different purposes; to use the technique effectively, the specific function of the question should be clear in the questioner's mind.

Your response to the above activity might include:

- To test for existing knowledge. This could be finding out what learners already know and bring to the session with them – important as you would wish to build upon this
- To check if learners are acquiring the new knowledge you present to them – feedback to you the teacher
- To motivate learners by giving them the opportunity to demonstrate their learning, or, alternatively, making them aware of their learning – feedback to the learners
- To encourage participation and involvement in the session – important if you wish to promote active learning
- To use learners and the diversity of the group as a resource
- To build up knowledge step by step or guide learners towards the answers you require
- To stimulate curiosity and encourage thought
- To maintain attention
- To let learners know that you are interested in them and their views and that they can learn from each other by sharing these
- To encourage divergent thinking.

Knowing why we ask questions is important, as our purpose will determine both the type of questions we ask and the way in which we ask them. The skills in using question and answer technique fall into two parts:

- Asking questions
- Dealing with the responses.

Asking questions

Sometimes the questions we ask will be seeking specific information from learners; we may want to test their knowledge, focus attention on particular aspects of the skill in question or build up knowledge in a step-by-step fashion through questioning rather than telling. If this is the case, we will use closed questions that point the learner towards the desired response. This sounds simple enough, but in practice is not always that easy.

Closed questions have to be sufficiently narrow to give the learner some indication of the type of answer we are looking for. We may not get an answer to our question simply because the question is too general or vague rather than because learners do not know the answer. Equally, however, the question must not be so 'closed' that the answer is obvious and there is no challenge in providing it. When using closed questions, we first identify the answer that we are looking for and then devise a question that will draw out this answer.

On other occasions we may want to find out what the learner thinks, what their views and perceptions are, or we may wish them to consider an issue or come up with a variety of ideas around a specific topic. We may wish to initiate discussion, debate or divergent thinking. In this case we do not wish to guide learners towards a predetermined answer or indeed to influence their answer at all, but to allow them to think creatively and express themselves freely. We are likely to be posing questions that encourage learners to think more broadly about How? Why? Where? When? and What? In this case, open questions are much more appropriate.

Once we have decided whether our questions will be closed or open, we need to consider which learners we want to answer the question. Will we encourage everyone to offer a response or direct specific learners to respond? General questioning consists of asking questions of the group as a whole. You could consider this as non-threatening in its approach, as learners have the option of answering or not. Whilst this sounds a good idea, the effectiveness of this approach can be questioned on a number of grounds:

- Less confident learners can be reluctant to participate
- More confident learners can dominate
- Individual responses can be missed by the group as a whole unless we repeat them
- We often make assumptions on behalf of the group as a whole based on the answers of individual learners.

Many of these limitations can be overcome by the use of directed questions. Directed questioning involves the teacher nominating the person who is to answer thus allowing questions to be distributed around the group as a whole, giving all learners an opportunity to answer. This offers an opportunity for a differentiated approach. Learners can be asked specific questions that are within their ability to respond to, but still constitute a challenge. More able and confident learners can be asked more difficult or abstract questions, whilst less able or less confident learners can be given less complex questions or questions that require them to recount an experience and that are descriptive rather than analytical. A good teacher will use their knowledge of their learners and their respective capabilities, taking account of body language, when deciding where to allocate a particular question. If, during a question and answer session, a learner suddenly finds a speck of dust on their shoe or an unsightly mark on the ceiling that demands their attention, it might be better to direct that question to someone else!

Dealing with responses

The responses to questions tend to fall into one of four categories:

1.   Correct answers

This is the most straightforward case. A correct answer suggests that the question was well framed and within learners' capacity to answer. This is a situation we would like to encourage so we reward correct answers with acknowledgement and praise. It may be appropriate to repeat the answer to ensure everyone has heard. This also allows the opportunity to rephrase the answer a little to make sure it aids learning exactly as we want it to.

> Well done John, that was an excellent answer. What John said was.....

2.   Partially correct answers

It is important to first give credit for the part of the answer that is correct before going on to deal with the part that is incorrect. This can be achieved in a number of ways but perhaps the most effective is to ask if anyone wants to add to it. The appropriate response will normally be provided by other learners. If no alternative explanation is forthcoming, we can offer it ourselves.

> Thank you, I liked the first part of your answer but I'm not sure about the second part. What do the rest of you think?
> Has anyone.....

3.   Incorrect answers

An incorrect answer can arise from a lack of knowledge, misinterpretation of the question or perhaps from the poor framing of the question itself. Whatever the reason, we don't wish to discourage learners from answering again. We therefore need to reply in a supportive manner. Subsequent shorter closed questions could be asked to lead the learner to the required answer or the question could be redirected. We should not leave other learners in any doubt about the correct answer to our questions. To maintain learner confidence, they could be asked another question that we are confident they can answer, fairly soon afterwards.

> I can see why you say that, but.....

> That's a good point but it doesn't really address the question

4. **No answer at all**

The lack of a response, even after redirecting, calls for a rephrasing of the question or breaking it down into smaller, simpler components. This will hopefully identify the cause of the lack of response. It may be that the subject of the question needs to be retaught, but alternatively it may be that you have not framed the question well. Avoid answering your own questions!

As a rule, it is best to repeat the responses to questions to the whole group to ensure everyone has heard.

The following checklist can be used to 'polish' your questioning technique.

☑ Ask simple questions first to encourage responses and build confidence.
☑ Allow learners time to absorb the question and formulate a response.
☑ Ensure all learners can hear both the question and the answer.
☑ Avoid asking questions of learners if we know they cannot answer. Eye contact, or the lack of it, will help in this respect.
☑ Recognise that broad or vague questions will invite a variety of answers.
☑ Praise correct answers; when correcting wrong answers try to find something positive in them.

Skill-based subjects

Skills can take many different forms; for example, social skills, Functional Skills, intellectual skills. Whilst the techniques referred to in this section could be applied to a greater or lesser extent to all of these, the focus will be on the teaching and acquisition of practical skills. First we will examine the nature of a skill itself and its performance. One definition of skill is:

An organised pattern of mental and/or physical activity.

This definition suggests that there is a 'knowledge' part to a skill and a 'doing' part, and such skills are generally referred to as 'psychomotor'. The balance of these components varies in different skills. Riding a bicycle, for instance, will have a greater 'doing' component, whereas using a computer will have a greater 'knowledge' component, but *all* skills will have elements of each. Once a skill has been mastered, it will be performed in a smooth, confident manner and with an economy of movement which keeps fatigue at bay even if the skill is performed for a substantial period of time. A good quality end product will be achieved reasonably quickly and with little wastage of materials.

If you are involved in the teaching of skills you will yourself be a 'skilled performer' and so will exhibit the above characteristics. By the time we have become skilled, most of what we do has become automatic; we do not have to think about it. Because of this we may not even be aware of all of the actions that we make. When we teach skills, it is easy to forget all that is involved and make a number of assumptions, concerning the nature of the skill itself and the readiness of the learners.

Skills analysis

To overcome the making of assumptions, the first stage in teaching a skill is to break the skill down into its component parts so that we are aware of all that is involved and can pass this information on to our learners. This process is known as skills analysis. In analysing a skill we are looking to answer questions such as:

- What are the specific actions involved in the skill?
- What is the exact sequence?
- What information is taken in through the senses at each stage?
- What decisions have to be made in the execution of the skill?
- What specific difficulties are associated with this particular skill?

In arriving at the answers to questions such as these, we first break the skill down into a number of smaller sub-skills. Each sub-skill is then broken down further until a level of detail appropriate to the existing knowledge and experience of learners is reached. In teaching a skill like bicycle riding, the breakdown could be:

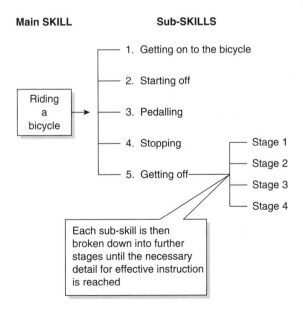

Activity 8.3

Think of a skill that you currently teach or could teach. Conduct a skills analysis as shown above.

Having analysed the skill we can use the results to consider the best way to demonstrate the skill to our learners. Generally, we use demonstration to impart the 'knowledge' component of a skill and some kind of practical activity or practice session for learners to consolidate this 'knowledge' and then acquire the 'doing' component. A typical skills session will contain both of these activities, the nature of the skill determining the relative amounts of each.

Demonstration

One of the most important factors to remember when giving a demonstration is that not only are you showing learners what to do in the performance of the particular skill, you are also showing them how to go about it. It is therefore essential to consider not only the content, but also the attitudes which you display when carrying out the demonstration. These might be attitudes towards issues of safety, hygiene or standards of work. It is easy to fall into a 'do as I say, not as I do' frame of mind, but what learners should be exposed to is good practice incorporating correct attitudes. A good demonstration exhibits the following positive features:

- It allows us to give a concrete example
- We can show how theory and practice link
- As demonstration is visual it is more easily understood and we can hold learners' attention more effectively
- We show correct practice – method, movement, pace.

Preparation

The secret of a good demonstration is the same as for most activities – good preparation and planning. This will involve:

Preparation of learners

☑ Making sure learners know the purpose of the demonstration and any specific points on which to focus.

Preparation of self

☑ Conducting a skills analysis to ensure clear guidance and a comprehensive commentary are given.
☑ Deciding how much of the skill is to be demonstrated at one time and arriving at an overall strategy for carrying out the demonstration.

Preparation of environment

☑ Making sure that everyone will be able to see and hear.
☑ Considering whether the demonstration is best observed from the front or from behind.
☑ Deciding whether to demonstrate to the whole group or whether to split them up into smaller groups and demonstrate to each group in turn.
☑ Consideration of health and safety issues.

Preparation of materials and equipment

☑ Making sure you have sufficient quantities of the correct materials.
☑ Ensuring all the equipment to be used is in good working order.
☑ Arranging for technician support if required.

Performing the demonstration

When we give a demonstration the sequence of 'whole, parts, whole' is often used. First the whole skill is demonstrated as a skilled performance. This attracts and focuses attention but also allows the learner to acquire a 'feel' for the complete skill and subsequently identify how the different parts of the skill fit together. There is a danger at this stage, however, that learners may be intimidated by a lengthy, perfect performance, leading to thoughts of 'I will never be able to do that!'. The complexity of the skill and previous experience and confidence of the learners should be considered when deciding how best to carry out the initial 'whole' demonstration.

The skill can then be broken into the sub-skills resulting from the skills analysis. Each of these is demonstrated, with explanation, at a pace that allows the learners to appreciate what it entails. The accompanying commentary or explanation will direct learners' attention to specific actions, but may not focus exclusively on the 'how to do' parts of a skill but might also give reasons as to the 'why'. There may also be some highlighting of the use of the senses in the particular skill:

Sight:	'if you watch for ...', 'at this stage you will probably see ...'
Hearing:	'if you hear ... you will know that ...', 'you should listen carefully to ...'
Touch:	'a light but firm grasp is needed ...', 'if you grasp it too tightly ...'
Taste:	'... normally produces a taste like ...', 'if it tastes of ... you will know that ...'
Smell:	'it should now smell like ...', 'note this particular smell. It means that ...'

Although in some skills the role of a particular sense may be greater (for example, in cooking: taste and smell; pottery: touch; music: hearing and touch) all skills have some kind of sensory input, and drawing learners' attention to this gives a greater feel and understanding of the skill in question.

We can make the demonstration more participative and more of an 'active learning' experience at this stage by involving learners through the use of questioning. Questions can ask learners to:

Explain:	'how can this be done?'
Predict:	'what do you think comes next?'
Analyse:	'why do you think I did that at this point?' or
Summarise:	'what were the first three things I did in this demonstration?'

Finally, we would demonstrate the whole skill again at a competent pace reinforcing all that we have previously demonstrated.

Practising the skill

Classroom management and the maintenance of an orderly environment are important in any kind of teaching that we undertake, but in a practical situation this becomes an even more important consideration as inappropriate behaviour can lead to serious consequences. Practical classes need to be started off in a controlled and organised manner. This is best achieved by initially gathering the group together in a convenient spot and addressing them as a whole. Clothing and equipment can be checked, and health and safety considerations reinforced, along with ground rules for this particular session. More practical matters such as time limits and procedures for the session – working singly or in pairs, expectations of progress, and use of tools, can then be covered before learners start work.

Once learners have started the practice session, our main role is that of monitoring individual progress and giving feedback, making sure learners know how they are getting on. This initially involves ensuring that everyone is using the correct technique to carry out the skill, and intervening when learners are having difficulty or are using incorrect methods. This may involve us in using 'on the spot' mini demonstrations, questioning or using the performance of other learners to guide individuals back onto the correct track.

When we have achieved this, monitoring becomes much more a case of checking progress and ensuring all learners remain engaged despite different rates of development. We need to give extra thought to those learners who acquire the skill more quickly, to ensure that they remain involved and challenged. We can achieve this by suggesting different contexts or problem-solving scenarios to extend their use of the skill. Ways to develop further can be agreed with individual learners to encourage further improvement and to cater for the range of aptitudes within the group. Similarly, we need to consider the needs of those learners who find acquisition of the skill more difficult, and therefore progress at a slower rate. Perhaps it will be necessary to set short-term goals or targets in such cases as part of the differentiation process.

Giving feedback

It is important to learners to know how they are doing whilst acquiring a skill so feedback is an essential part of the practice element of acquiring a skill. Good feedback acknowledges what the learner is doing correctly and identifies clearly and concisely what can be done to further improve performance. Good feedback also incorporates appropriate use of praise, particularly important for learners to whom the acquisition of the skill does not come that easily. Motivation is extremely important in the process of skills acquisition, and when a learner has been progressing well it can be frustrating when improvement begins to slow down. This can frequently happen; learners can improve their performance rapidly to begin with but then tend to 'plateau' as the skill is consolidated. Learners often need to be helped through this time of apparently slow progress.

The way in which we give feedback can also encourage either learner dependence or independence. There are essentially two styles that can be employed;

either **telling**:

> That's good so far although you might have ... just try that and when you have finished, let me know and I'll come back and check it for you.

or **asking**:

> That's interesting – why did you do it that way? Do you think it's the best way? Can you see a different approach? What do you think you need to do next?

'Telling' is quicker, to the point, and gives confidence to learners, especially if they have limited experience in using the particular skill. These are important considerations when you have a number of learners to attend to and a limited time in which to achieve this. Learners may still be unsure of themselves and their capabilities and appreciate straightforward advice and guidance. Potentially, however, when the teacher is no longer there to give advice and guidance, confidence disappears and so 'telling' can lead to dependence on the teacher.

'Asking', on the other hand, invites learners to self-evaluate progress and arrive at their own conclusions, thus making them much more independent. Learners may, however, see this approach as intimidating, particularly if they are limited in their ability to analyse and evaluate.

Which approach to use then? Some learners can cope with a more provocative or challenging method of questioning, whereas others may require a more supportive approach. We use a combination of the two approaches or whichever is the most appropriate in a given circumstance. As a general rule we should try to 'wean' learners away from reliance on the teacher and help them to become more independent in their learning and performance of the skill.

 Activity 8.4

Can you think of any other strategies you could use to promote learner independence?

Attitudinally-based subjects

Unless your subject is one of those directly concerned with attitude change, there can be a tendency to neglect this area, concentrating instead on the knowledge or skills to be taught and which are uppermost in your mind. This is partly because attitude change is a long-term rather than a single session objective, but nevertheless it applies at some level in all subjects. Perhaps you teach practical skills and would like to change learners' attitudes towards theory classes; if you teach plumbing or catering you may be concerned about attitudes to accuracy or careful presentation. You may teach Functional Skills and have to overcome negative attitudes towards the subject itself. Maybe you work in a laboratory or workshop setting and need to address attitudes towards safety. Perhaps, in the groups you teach, bullying or making fun of others takes place and what you need to address is learners' attitudes towards each other. Possibly it is learners' attitudes to standards of work that you wish to challenge or maybe even attitudes towards themselves. The list is fairly long and hopefully you agree that attitudes are important in all aspects of learning, irrespective of subject.

Activity 8.5

Identify an attitude displayed by your learners that you would like to influence. Bear this attitude in mind as you read the remainder of the chapter and see which strategies you might employ to achieve this.

The structure of an attitude

Attitudes themselves can be thought of as being made up of three separate but related parts:

1 **Beliefs:** We have some knowledge of whatever it is we hold an attitude towards, acquired either from our own experience or some other source. The knowledge that informs your attitude towards asylum seekers, for instance, may come either from being an asylum seeker, from having had contact with an asylum seeker, having read about asylum seekers in the newspapers or from having seen a programme on TV. This knowledge then may be first-hand or second-hand, but whichever it is, it is open to interpretation. It is what we believe to be the case based on our selection from the facts or experiences to which we have been exposed. For this reason it is called our belief.

2 **Feelings:** Suppose you have a strong, negative attitude towards drinking and driving. Upon hearing of a case where a drink driver has caused a serious accident but you perceive the person has 'got away with' a fine in court rather than a prison sentence, you may well be angry. This second component of an attitude concerns not what we believe we know about the subject of our attitude but how it makes us feel. Anything towards which we hold an attitude will evoke an emotional response or 'gut feeling'. The intensity of the feeling will depend upon how strongly we hold the attitude in question.

3 **Actions:** How would we know what attitude you hold towards dogs? If you were approached by a large, boisterous dog and you smiled and went to stroke it, we would know your attitude was positive. If, on the other hand, you looked uncomfortable or crossed the road to avoid the dog, it would be reasonable to assume your attitude was less than positive. Our actions – what we do (or do not do) – form the third component of an attitude.

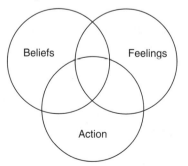

Together these three components make up the whole attitude. We can represent this as in the diagram above.

Some approaches to bringing about attitude change focus on the third of these components – the action. An example of trying to achieve attitude change towards drinking and driving through affecting the action component can be seen in random breath testing and the resulting consequences of failing or passing. In an educational setting we might give penalties for handing in work late or some kind of reward for consistent punctuality. It could be argued, however, that compliance rather than attitude change is all that is being achieved.

In a teaching situation we would normally try to influence one of the other two components of the attitude – the beliefs or feelings. If we consider beliefs first, we could bring about change by altering the information base on which the beliefs are held, telling people what the appropriate beliefs are so they would also adopt them. Telling, however, only has a limited effect. We hold more strongly to a new belief when we arrive at it ourselves rather than being told by others; this can be achieved by using active methods such as discussion.

Discussion

The purpose of discussion as a learning activity is the exchange of knowledge, ideas and opinions in order to arrive at some form of conclusion. Appropriate topics for a discussion would therefore be based around issues rather than facts as the intention is to raise awareness, solve problems, explore issues or make decisions. In order to be effective as a learning activity, those taking part in the discussion need to possess a certain level of knowledge on the chosen topic and the process has to be carefully managed to ensure focus is maintained.

As a learning activity, discussion has a number of positive features:
- Learners are encouraged to actively contribute to the session, share experience and learn from others
- Learners can explore ideas in a safe and secure setting, allowing them to gain clearer understanding and reconsider their views
- Learners can gain in self confidence
- Learners have opportunities to exhibit their knowledge
- Learners can assimilate information together, which encourages the process of group formation
- We get an indication of the level of understanding within the group
- Agreement within the group can be achieved around given issues.

Equally, discussion can have a number of limitations. Most of these relate to the participants themselves. Some prefer to be 'taught' and do not find it easy to participate in discussion. Some may try to dominate the discussion whilst others may opt out. Some may not take the activity seriously and others may miss the point altogether or deviate from the topic under discussion in their contributions. Most of these particular limitations can be overcome, however, by effective management of the group and of the discussion.

 Activity 8.6

Think back to some past experience of discussion method where you may have learnt very little or even nothing at all. Jot down a few notes on why this was so and what could have been done to improve the situation.

Now do the same for an effective discussion – where you or group members learned a lot, were successful, enjoyed it and were interested. What was it that made it so good?

In your reflections on ineffective discussions you may well have identified a lack of clarity over what was being discussed and a lack of shared purpose as being root causes. Often, however, the reason can be much simpler and lie in the arrangement of the furniture in the room. It is difficult to discuss, for instance, when the group are sitting in rows. Informality and all-round eye contact are essential for productive and inclusive discussion, and this is normally achieved by placing chairs in circles, preferably without tables or any other physical barriers to communication.

Another possible danger is that of learners 'pooling ignorance' – perhaps making inappropriate comments or lines of argument or maybe reinforcing undesirable stereotypes. In this instance it might be wise to participate in or lead the discussion rather than let it proceed down an unproductive path. Although a discussion may be open-ended it will nonetheless have a purpose; some management or leading of the discussion may be necessary to make sure this is achieved.

In the case of attitude change, however, discussion is intended to challenge existing beliefs and ideas. In order for this to be achieved, these must be expressed in the first place. The process of querying and challenging needs to be carefully handled, as the beliefs that learners will hold most strongly arise out of their own experiences and are based on conclusions they themselves have reached. Challenges to these beliefs can be taken personally. An objective approach has to be taken, based on questioning and presentation of evidence for discussion. Good leadership of a discussion also involves summarising at frequent intervals, particularly at the end. In the case of attitude change, summaries should be prefaced by 'so what you are telling me' or 'what we seem to be agreeing on' to reinforce the notion that conclusions have come from the group and the process of discussion rather than from the teacher.

There are a number of ways in which we can make discussion more productive and more likely to serve its intended purpose:

Discussion is most effective when we have a clear agreed purpose in mind and a subject that lends itself to some form of deliberation

- ☑ Make sure the choice of topic is relevant and allows scope for discussion.
- ☑ Ensure everyone is aware of the purpose of the discussion.
- ☑ Consider supplying some 'trigger' materials such as a short DVD or video clip, case study or newspaper article to contextualise and give an initial focus.

Discussion is most effective when everyone feels a part of the process and their contributions matter

- ☑ Set ground rules for the discussion.
- ☑ Use verbal or non-verbal cues to encourage active listening and dispel competitiveness.
- ☑ Use questions to direct and redirect and to encourage participation.
- ☑ Acknowledge contributions.
- ☑ Avoid expressing own views; try and act as 'neutral chairperson'.

Discussion is more effective when some definite conclusions are drawn

- ☑ Control the pace of discussion allowing time for response and reflection.
- ☑ If necessary, break up the discussion into smaller segments.
- ☑ Keep discussion focused and limit digression.
- ☑ Summarise throughout the discussion at appropriate points.
- ☑ Help individuals or groups to identify what has been learned and how it might affect attitudes in the future.

Role play

If we turn now to bringing about attitude change by affecting the 'feelings' component of an attitude, one effective activity we can use is role play. Role play involves a learner or learners acting and behaving as another person might in a given situation and experiencing the feelings associated with this. It allows experience of a situation or practice of a technique or skill in a safe environment, where mistakes can be made without fear and learned from.

Activity 8.7

List the various role plays you have used or come across. What was the purpose of each?

Role play can have one of several functions, depending upon the context in which it is used:

- To demonstrate or model a given behaviour, for example a receptionist in a hotel greeting a guest
- To practice a skill, for example buying a train ticket in a language class
- To review and analyse our actions, for example in sports coaching
- To encourage creativity, for example acting out a fantasy in a drama class
- To explore the feelings aroused in a given situation, for example in diversity training
- To gain empathy, for example being blindfolded in order to identify with learners who are visually impaired.

It is role play used with the last two kinds of intention that we will be focusing on in this chapter. We will be asking learners to 'walk in the other person's moccasins' as the North American Indians would say, in order to experience what others have felt. We hope that in doing this we will have an effect on the 'feelings' component of an existing attitude.

It is important to note at this stage that in this type of role play you will not be dealing with the logic and certainty of knowledge or facts, but with emotions that can sometimes be quite intense. Reactions can be unpredictable and managing this kind of activity requires its own particular skills and sensitivity. If you are new to role play it is a good idea to observe another teacher running one before trying it out yourself. It is not an activity to be used lightly and needs careful planning, which can be considered under the following headings.

Initial planning

As with all learning activities, you should give careful thought not only to identifying exactly what it is that the role play is to achieve but also to the characteristics of the group and individuals within the group with whom you intend to use the activity.

Considering the *exact purpose* of the role play will help you to make decisions about devising the role play itself and how best to manage the feedback session at the end of the exercise. The purpose will shape your answers to questions like:

- What kind of scenario will provide the desired experience but still be considered realistic? How many roles will be involved?
- How much time needs to be allocated to acting out the role play and how much for the feedback at the end?
- How should feedback be structured? Who should speak first – role players, others in the group, teacher?
- Should roles be allocated or should they be voluntary? Do role players need to be briefed before the session? Should the briefing take place by talking to participants or by giving them role cards or both?

Considering the **nature of the group** will help to decide how to run the activity and will answer questions like:

- Is the group sufficiently mature and confident to benefit from this type of activity? Have they used role play before? If so, how did it go and what can be learned from the previous experience?
- Are there particularly sensitive learners in this group I may have to watch out for?
- Are there particular learners who, for some good reason, I do or do not want to take on roles or to work together?
- Will the group benefit more from conducting the role play in one large group or splitting up into smaller groups?

Running the role play

We can now consider the practicalities, one of which is how to introduce the activity. Not all learners find role play to be a comfortable experience and so there can be resistance to the notion of role play. It may, therefore, be necessary to think of a non-threatening method of presenting the session to the group. This can be as straightforward as not using the term 'role play', but simply giving an overview of the activity and its purpose.

The next stage is to give an overview of the chosen scenario before briefing anyone to whom a role has been allocated. How this is done will depend upon the situation, but often some form of written instruction works well. Participants will probably require a little time to prepare themselves and small groups can be used to help in this. At this stage it may be worth briefing the rest of the group, as, although they may not be allocated a role, they nonetheless have an important part to play. Perhaps there are particular issues or factors they can be alerted to, or specific responses you would particularly like them to look out for.

Once everyone is ready, the activity can commence within previously set time limits.

The debrief

Arguably, this is the most important part of the activity. Role play is an example of an experiential approach and learning only occurs through reflection on and analysis of the experience. A well managed debrief is crucial if learning, and therefore attitude change, is to occur.

At its conclusion, you need to formally end the role play as a signal to the participants to step out of role and return to being 'their normal selves'. When this has been achieved and the attention of the group as a whole has been captured, a structured discussion can begin. One way of achieving this is to consider:

- What actually happened – what did observers see, what did role players feel?
- Some analysis – why do we think ..., how did that ...?
- What has been learned – what has been gained from the experience, what has been discovered, what are the implications?

Finally, learners need to take what has been learned and, formally or informally, arrive at some kind of action plan relating to the attitudes they will display in the future.

Attitude change is not an instantaneous process – it has to be worked at over a period of time. Of the approaches suggested above, discussion is the more widely used and is certainly the more advisable approach if you are fairly new to teaching. Role play is a powerful method but can be unpredictable and difficult to manage.

Having looked at the different types of methods and activities that we can use within our different subject specialisms, the next chapter turns our attention to a consideration of the various ways we can support these through the effective use of resources.

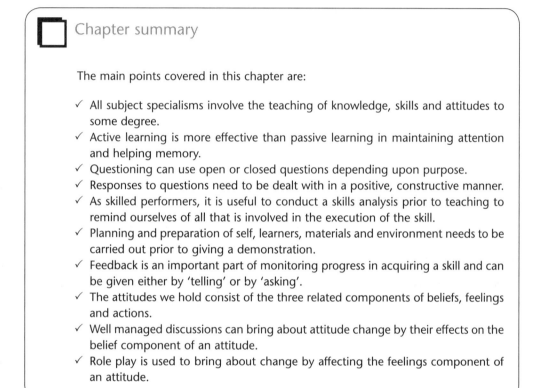

Chapter summary

The main points covered in this chapter are:

- ✓ All subject specialisms involve the teaching of knowledge, skills and attitudes to some degree.
- ✓ Active learning is more effective than passive learning in maintaining attention and helping memory.
- ✓ Questioning can use open or closed questions depending upon purpose.
- ✓ Responses to questions need to be dealt with in a positive, constructive manner.
- ✓ As skilled performers, it is useful to conduct a skills analysis prior to teaching to remind ourselves of all that is involved in the execution of the skill.
- ✓ Planning and preparation of self, learners, materials and environment needs to be carried out prior to giving a demonstration.
- ✓ Feedback is an important part of monitoring progress in acquiring a skill and can be given either by 'telling' or by 'asking'.
- ✓ The attitudes we hold consist of the three related components of beliefs, feelings and actions.
- ✓ Well managed discussions can bring about attitude change by their effects on the belief component of an attitude.
- ✓ Role play is used to bring about change by affecting the feelings component of an attitude.

→ Reference

Dale, E. (1969) *Audio Visual Methods in Teaching* (3rd edn). Orlando: Holt, Rinehart and Winston.

📖 Further reading

Bligh, D.A. (2000) *What's the Use of Lectures?* San Francisco: Jossey Bass.
Although a bit 'academic' in its tone, this book covers all the aspects of the lecture as a teaching method you could possibly want to know about. Chapters 18 and 19 give some ideas for using combinations of methods to give a more active approach overall.

Exley, K. and Dennick, R. (2009) *Giving a Lecture*. Routledge: London.

Hayes, N. (1993) *Principles of Social Psychology*. Hove: Lawrence Erlbaum Associates.
A social psychology text book, Chapter 5 of which gives a reasonably in depth but readable coverage of attitudes, defining terms and examining change and measurement.

Hillier, Y. (2011) *Reflective Teaching in Further and Adult Education* (2nd edn). London: Continuum.
A useful demonstration checklist can be found in Chapter 6.

Petty, G. (2009) *Teaching Today – A Practical Guide* (4th edn). Cheltenham: Nelson.
Chapter 13 discusses different aspects of demonstration and Chapter 16 explores issues related to the supervision of practical sessions.

Reece, I. and Walker, S. (2007) *Teaching, Training and Learning: A Practical Guide* (6th edn). Sunderland: Business Education Publishers.
Chapter 1 includes a section which looks specifically at planning for the teaching of skills and provides a good example of skills analysis.

Van Ments, M. (1999) *The Effective Use of Role Play* (2nd edn). London: Kogan Page.
This is the classic text on role play.

Useful websites

Active learning – overview by Geoff Petty along with links to suggestions for different activities
www.geoffpetty.com/activelearning.html

Lots of good examples of skills analysis – see 'How To Fold a T-Shirt In 2 Seconds – Explained' in particular
www.videojug.com/

Cognitive dissonance and attitude change – affecting the belief component of an attitude
http://changingminds.org/explanations/theories/cognitive_dissonance.htm

Effective use of resources

How resources support learning

Learning takes place as a result of connections being made in the brain. We cannot control this; it happens automatically. We do have some say, however, in how the information reaches the brain in the first place. Information is sent and received in a number of ways that use our various senses – through our eyes (sight), our ears (hearing) and through our other senses such as touch, taste and smell.

The proportion of information taken in by the senses will depend to some extent upon the nature of the activity in which we are engaged. Taste and smell, for instance, assume greater importance when cooking, and a potter working on a wheel would place a greater reliance on touch. Generally, however, we take in most information by sight. Research shows that the split is approximately:

> 80% through our eyes
> 15% through our ears
> 5% through our other senses

The reception of information can be affected by a number of factors as shown below.

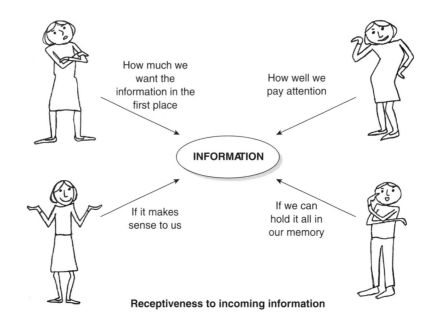

Receptiveness to incoming information

It is these factors that we can influence, and through effective use of resources we can:

Create interest: We add another dimension when senses other than hearing are brought into play. To be able to hear, see, touch and, maybe, even smell or taste what is being talked about brings the subject alive.

Attract and maintain attention: Visual resources, in particular, grab our attention. If you look at this page your eye will be drawn immediately to the diagram rather than any other part of the page. Visual material can provide a point of focus around which to structure information and highlight the most important points to be made.

Help understanding: The more senses we can bring to bear, the more clues we have to help us to interpret the object or information under examination.

Make it easier to remember: Generally we remember best if:

- We are interested in the information
- We focus attention fully on it
- We can understand it.

Resources help in all of these respects. There is a saying 'a picture paints a thousand words'. Visual resources act as pictures, reducing the bulk of information to be taken in.

The range of resources

If the use of resources promotes learning, we need to be aware of the resources we have at our disposal.

Activity 9.1

Make a list of all of the resources you currently use or could use.

You will have come up with a number of possibilities. For simplification, we can divide these into four categories:

1 Prepared visual and aural material, possibly using various projection devices, DVD, Internet sources, CD player, cassette recorder
2 Prepared written or diagrammatic material: textbooks, handouts, worksheets, charts, posters
3 Spontaneous recording on a whiteboard, electronic whiteboard, flip chart
4 Models or the 'real thing'.

You may find that most of your examples fall into one particular category depending on the type of teaching that you do, but you should be able to draw to a certain extent on all categories.

Using visual and aural material

In this first category we have a number of devices that allow us to use prepared resources. We can show slides, DVDs or videos we have made ourselves, or which may have been commercially produced, to illustrate a wide range of topics. Specific software packages obtainable on CD or by download may be available for the computer which can be linked to projection facilities. All of these are meant primarily for use with groups but can be used with individuals.

The list above contains a range of possibilities; you will doubtless have experienced a number of them.

Activity 9.2

Identify a specific teaching session in which you could use one new resource from this category.

Using written and diagrammatic material

The second category consists of prepared written or diagrammatic resources. Charts and posters on the wall liven up a teaching room and can be referred to specifically during a session, particularly if they have been produced by learners. Gapped handouts and worksheets can be used to guide learners systematically through the content of a teaching session. Textbooks can provide a useful reference during a session as long as they are used to supplement, not guide, the teaching that is taking place. Handouts can provide a useful summary of content.

 **Activity 9.3**

How could you extend the range of resources you use from this category?

Using resources spontaneously

The third category is concerned with resources we would use when recording or illustrating thoughts as we progress through a teaching session. The whiteboard, electronic whiteboard and flip chart are most useful for jotting down themes, ideas and examples. Contributions from the group can be recognised and recorded and subsequently presented in an organised format. Resources falling into this category are generally used in a more spontaneous manner; we would generally write on them, or invite learners to write or draw upon them, although there can be some preparation beforehand, particularly in the case of the flip chart.

Activity 9.4

What new use can you make of such resources?

Using models or the 'real thing'

All of the above, however, are substitutes for our fourth category, the 'real thing'. We cannot always introduce real items into the teaching environment. Introducing a plumbing system, a real body to resuscitate, a heart, or the latest machine, may be impracticable for reasons such as size, safety, availability or cost; this is where we turn to other resources as a substitute. When it is possible to use the 'real thing' or alternatively a model, the impact is greater because the world we are learning about has been introduced into the session. The impact is even greater if the item can be passed round, touched, examined, and invariably generates the kind of interest and discussion that other visual aids do not.

So, there is a variety of options available to us. Appropriate use of these will give our teaching interest and variety.

Designing resources for impact and purpose

To make the most of the resources you have selected, you will need to think about the best designs and the most effective ways to use them. Some simple rules that apply to the use of all types of resource are:

- Resources should be used both appropriately and sparingly. They are intended to support, not lead learning. The intention is to enhance the message we are putting across, not distract from it.
- Ensure the resources you use reflect the diversity and experience of learners.
- Always check equipment is working before using it and ensure you know how to operate it properly. Have a standby in case of equipment failure.

The majority of the resources we use are visual in nature. Often, visual aids are used to help learners to process information, such as drawing attention to the important points and organising these in such a way that makes it easier for learners to commit them to memory. This is usually the case both when we record information spontaneously, as with the whiteboard, electronic board or flip chart, and when we prepare it in advance, as with projected material such as PowerPoint slides.

Some of the more useful visual design techniques are illustrated below.

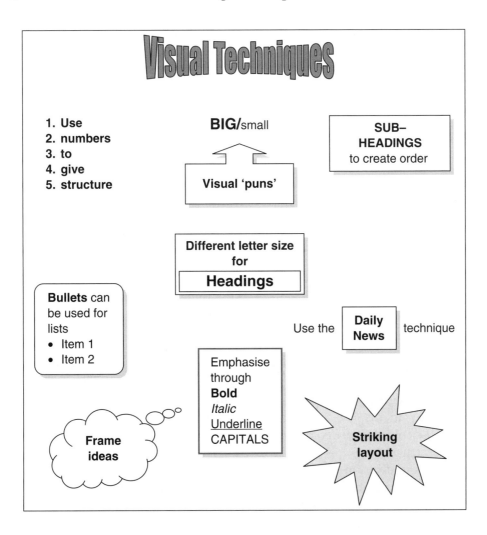

Generally, when considering any type of visual aid:

- Use lots of space – avoid cluttering the visual with too much information
- Use colours to emphasise key points
- Remember lower case is easier to read than UPPER CASE
- Make sure all words and illustrations are large enough to be seen by everyone in the room.

Making effective use of resources

We turn now to making best use of the resources we have at our disposal. Information and Communication Technology (ICT) is playing an increasingly important role both as a resource itself, and in the production of the more traditional visual aids. Word processing and the storing and importing of different types of images allow the production of better quality and more effective visual aids, such as handouts and slides, giving a more professional finish and appearance.

Computerised projection systems enable us to access the Internet on an individual or group basis. Other possibilities have developed as multimedia software packages and IT facilities become more widely available in the classroom. As yet, however, access to such technologies within many teaching environments is still fairly limited, and so we will be concentrating first on the more commonly available resources and visual aids before examining the possibilities that are opened up to us by electronic means.

1. Whiteboard

The whiteboard is a modern, cleaner, easier to use version of the old school chalkboard and fulfils much the same purpose. We would normally use whiteboards during teaching to:

- Record the main points or headings of the material we are covering
- Illustrate and clarify more complex or technical points
- Record responses and contributions from learners.

We can prepare work in advance on a whiteboard, but flip charts or PowerPoint slides are more suitable for this purpose. When the whiteboard is used in a spontaneous manner, however, we can still have some idea in advance of the most effective way to display the information; will we group certain contributions together, use columns, use colours to highlight, bullets to add emphasis or headings to provide structure?

Whatever our decisions regarding display, our writing on a board needs to be tidy and large enough to be seen from all parts of the room. Achieving this, however, usually requires practice, as there is a tendency for writing to tail off across the board.

It can be useful to mentally divide the board into two or three vertical segments and use these one at a time. When we have finished focusing on the whiteboard, we should clean it, otherwise it may distract learners from what we are moving on to next. This does mean that we have no permanent record of what has been done and this is the main disadvantage of using the whiteboard.

2. Flip chart

We can use a flip chart to fulfil all the same functions as a whiteboard, although the flip chart is considerably smaller and will therefore hold less information at one time.

The additional advantage of the flip chart, as we mentioned earlier, is that we can use it to prepare information and diagrams in advance. Such prepared material, however, can act as a distraction if learners can see it before it is required. To maximise impact and avoid distraction we can use a blank sheet between prepared pages, giving the same effect as cleaning the whiteboard.

If we do not wish to display all of the information at one time, we can attach a blank flip chart sheet to the top of the page containing the information. We are then able to display the information gradually as and when appropriate.

The flip chart has additional potential as a teaching resource as we can detach individual sheets from it and groups of learners can use these to work on. The results can be displayed on the walls, allowing further discussion of the points they contain. A variation on this theme is when flip chart sheets with headings are placed around the teaching room and learners circulate, recording comments and ideas. This can then be used as the basis for group discussion.

3. Handouts

During any teaching session, learners will often want to try to remember as much as possible of the information given. They cannot commit everything to memory and so will take notes whilst we are talking to them or copy information from the whiteboard, flip chart or whatever visual aid we happen to be using. This creates problems with attention, which is now divided between two different sources.

As we are aware of this, we might give out handouts that provide an accurate record of the session; these can be taken away, therefore freeing learners from the need to take copious notes. We do not have to provide an exact transcript of the session and may even simply copy the presentation we are using. Handouts which fulfil this function are known as summary handouts and so we would normally give them out at the end of the teaching session.

We can also use summary handouts to introduce topics and refer to them as the session progresses. In this case we would distribute them at the beginning of or at some appropriate point during the teaching session. Because they are used in a relatively passive manner, however, these are the type of handout that are often filed away and never referred to again, or are even left behind in the teaching room.

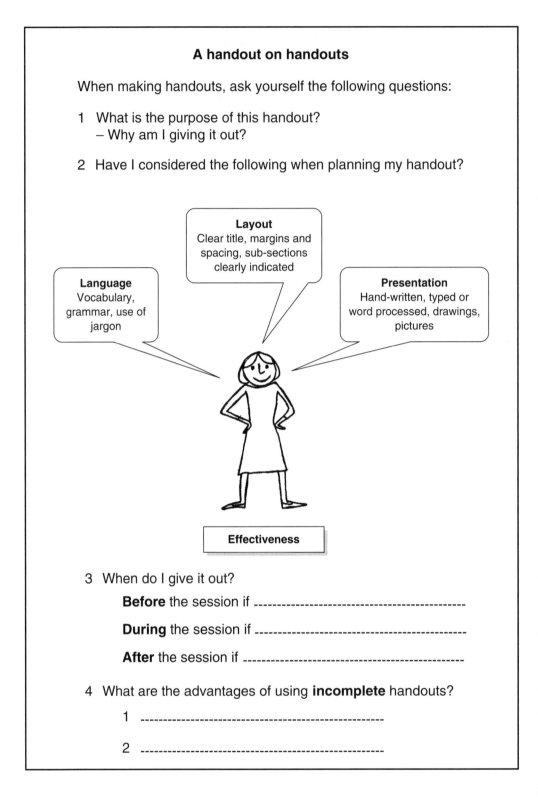

A handout on handouts

When making handouts, ask yourself the following questions:

1 What is the purpose of this handout?
– Why am I giving it out?

2 Have I considered the following when planning my handout?

Language
Vocabulary, grammar, use of jargon

Layout
Clear title, margins and spacing, sub-sections clearly indicated

Presentation
Hand-written, typed or word processed, drawings, pictures

Effectiveness

3 When do I give it out?

Before the session if --

During the session if --

After the session if --

4 What are the advantages of using **incomplete** handouts?

1 ---

2 ---

An alternative approach is to use the incomplete or gapped handout with blank spaces for learners to fill in. This has the advantage that it allows a structured set of notes to be taken away, but it also involves the learner in an active consideration of the information rather than merely passively recording it. In this way we can make the handout part of the teaching session rather than an extra, and it is more likely to be referred back to at a later stage. It can provide a memory aid, not just for the information it contains, but also for the teaching session as a whole.

As well as using gapped handouts for recording information, we can use them to:

- Test initial knowledge levels
- Promote discussion
- Test understanding in the session
- Encourage learners to arrive at solutions to problems
- Review previous experiences related to the current session
- Apply what has been learned
- Provide structure to group work.

The presentation of handouts, as with other resources, can greatly enhance their effectiveness. Images from the Internet can be used to increase visual impact and tables help in presenting information in an organised and more easily understood manner. To make best use of handouts, refer to the 'handout' opposite.

4. Overhead projector

The overhead projector (OHP) is, quite simply, a machine that projects images onto a screen from a transparent film placed on top of it. It is used less frequently nowadays having been superseded by more modern projection systems such as PowerPoint, which is discussed later. A lot of the principles behind use of the OHP, however, apply also to the newer systems, and it is worth briefly reminding ourselves of these. The primary purpose of the OHP is often to highlight the *main points* of an explanation or session as a whole. About six lines of text on a single transparency are therefore regarded as sufficient; maximum effect is achieved by using the techniques of reveal and overlays.

Reveal
This technique allows control over the rate at which information is presented by simply placing a piece of paper, or preferably card, over the top of the transparency and pulling it down gradually to 'reveal' information at the appropriate moment.

If all of the information is presented to learners in one go, it may well prove to be a distraction. On a list, for example, while the first item is being explained, learner attention may well have been focused on reading and wondering about the subsequent items. Revealing the items gradually helps focus attention in the appropriate place.

Overlay

Information regarded as too complex to be presented all at once, is broken down into smaller, more easily understood chunks, each on a separate transparency. Laying the transparencies on top of each other allows a gradual increase in complexity to be achieved, thus helping understanding.

The principles which underpin reveal and overlay can be applied by using the animation tools in PowerPoint.

E-resources

PowerPoint presentations

PowerPoint is part of the Microsoft Office suite and is a program that allows you to create presentations with text, graphics, hyperlinks and sound, displayed on a sequence of individual slides. Once the basic techniques of slide production have been mastered, it can be used to generate presentations quite quickly and easily. These can be stored systematically and modified electronically. By going to the 'print' mode, handouts, in a variety of formats, 'speaker's notes' and outlines can be printed, as well as copies of the original slides.

PowerPoint has its origins in industry, where presentations were made in the boardroom. Its purpose was to present the greatest amount of information in the shortest time to a specific and knowledgeable group. So, care has to be taken in adapting what is primarily a 'business system' into a learning environment; it has to be used in a different manner, as its purpose is to *support* learning and learning activities rather than *lead* a presentation. 'Death by PowerPoint' is now acknowledged as a major cause of fatalities in the learning environment.

We have already seen that the purpose of a visual aid is to attract and maintain attention, promote understanding and make it easier to commit material to memory.

As with the OHP:

- Slides should be simple and uncluttered and used to introduce, highlight or summarise rather than deliver large amounts of information.
- They should contain headings, short bulleted lists and visuals. As with the OHP the rate at which the content of each slide is displayed can be controlled. This can be achieved by using reveal and build effects, which are accessed through the Custom animation tab, and can be used to make text and pictures enter, exit or move. To avoid the presentation becoming a distraction, it can be left when it has served its immediate purpose and returned to when required by use of either the 'b' key on the keyboard (blanks out the screen and returns to the slide when pressed again) or the 'w' key (similar to 'b' key but turns the screen white).

PowerPoint can be operated directly from the computer keyboard by using the 'Enter' key. There are also a number of keyboard shortcuts which can be used to introduce additional functions; pressing the F1 key whilst running a slideshow will reveal these. The more useful shortcuts are:

PowerPoint shortcuts

Key	Function
N	next part of slide
P	returns to previous image
number key and 'enter'	takes you to that number slide in the presentation
'ctrl' plus 'a'	displays a pointer (normally an arrow)
'ctrl' plus 'h'	hides the pointer
'ctrl' plus 'p'	changes the arrow to a pen.

Using the keyboard to control PowerPoint means we have to be within touching distance of it, so wireless remote controls which allow us more mobility in the classroom are more commonly used. If used in conjunction with the interactive 'Smart Board', a similar effect can be achieved by tapping on the board surface.

Using hyperlinks, PowerPoint can be used to devise stand-alone learning packages which can be incorporated into Virtual Learning Environments (VLEs) (see below in this chapter).

PowerPoint, then, is a powerful resource but we need to remind ourselves that it is a visual *aid*. If we wish to use it to the best effect to aid learning it should complement rather than lead or dominate what we do.

If you are an Apple user, rather than a PC user, you can use 'Keynotes' a similar application to PowerPoint. If you upload your completed slideshow to iWork. com, it can then be downloaded in Keynote, PowerPoint or PDF format, giving compatibility with other systems (see web addresses at the end of this chapter).

An alternative presentation medium which is becoming increasingly popular is 'Prezi' (see web address at the end of this chapter). Prezis are created on a single 'canvas' rather than on a series of slides. Movement between the different items on the canvas is achieved by 'zooming' in and out from one to another which gives a more interesting and exciting visual display than the linear approach adopted by PowerPoint. Because of this method of display, however, it is not possible to print a complementary handout version for learners. A link to an example prezi on assertive discipline can be found at the end of this chapter.

The interactive whiteboard

An interactive whiteboard looks like, and can be used in the same way as, an ordinary whiteboard but has the added advantage that it connects to a computer and projector, allowing the computer's desktop to be displayed on the board's surface. The computer can be controlled from the board; the pen acts like a mouse. This means that not only can the Internet, PowerPoint, or any other application that can be accessed by computer be displayed on the whiteboard, but anything which is recorded onto the whiteboard can be transferred to the computer and thus saved and retrieved for future use. This means that users, whether teacher or learner, can input both at the computer and at the board.

Different makes of whiteboard vary in their method of operation and come with different software and resources. Currently the two major suppliers in the UK are Promethean and Smartboard, and it is worth visiting their websites (see end of chapter for addresses) as both contain user forums and offer free resources. Under the government's 2005 'Harnessing Technology' policy, most schools in the country have interactive whiteboards in place. Resources are therefore mainly school-based but can be adapted for other age groups. What is significant here is that, due to exposure at an earlier stage of their educational experience, future lifelong learners will no doubt expect this technology as a norm.

Some of the common tools used include:

- Reveal blind: The tool will go up/down/left/right. It can be used for columns as well as for lists
- Spotlight: Reveals only a section of the content on the board. Its shape and size can be varied and it can be moved around the board. This allows attention to be focused on specific items
- Timer: A digital or analogue clock which can either count down or count up and sits in the corner of the board; good for allowing groups to self regulate the timing of group work
- Camera capture: Allows parts of text or images from any displayable source to be captured and placed on a new clean page for further discussion and annotation. This is especially useful when preparing lessons (copyright allowing).

It is important to remember that the whiteboard is interactive and not just a medium through which to route PowerPoint presentations – teachers and learners can use it either individually or collaboratively.

Examples of teacher-led use include:

- Using a variety of quiz-based applications as an informal assessment tool or starter activity
- Showing PowerPoint slides to supplement and illustrate information given
- Demonstrating skills such as completing calculations, filling in forms

- Viewing and surfing the Internet from the whiteboard to illustrate topical issues
- Showing video clips to initiate discussion, explain or show applications of new concepts
- Writing over the top of slides, diagrams or text to highlight and annotate points.

The above uses exploit only part of the potential of this resource and it is important to remember that the whiteboard is interactive; as well as being used by teachers, it can also be used by learners or collaboratively between the two. Examples of learner-led use include:

- Adding their contributions to a discussion by writing them directly on to the whiteboard
- Working in groups on Word documents or spreadsheets which can be displayed and discussed
- Contributing individually or in small groups to label diagrams, or create drawings or mind maps.

To make the whiteboards even more interactive, classroom response systems are now being linked to them, allowing for comprehensive, instant feedback from learners. The idea of the response system is that each learner has a handheld device like a remote control or small mobile phone. In its simplest mode this offers an A to F choice; as simple multi-choice questions come up on the interactive whiteboard, the group can respond. The responses are recorded by the whiteboard and can be viewed later either as a pie chart (anonymously) or by learner's name.

Results can also be exported to Excel for future analysis, and, if required, fed into a college's data management system for record keeping. As well as allowing responses to prepared material, the system can also be used spontaneously. At any point in the session questions can be written to the whiteboard and responses gained instantly.

Initial assessment of learners' levels of understanding can take place simply at the beginning of each session. Formative assessment can be carried out quickly and easily (see Chapter 10). It is relatively simple to give a 10-minute input then pose a few questions to help gauge whether learners have absorbed key points.

Opinions can be sought through questions such as 'Do you agree or disagree with the congestion charge?' Those who strongly agree can input 'A' and those who disagree input 'F'; those who have less strong opinions can choose somewhere in between. It then might be interesting to take a poll again at the end the discussion/debate to see if opinions have shifted. The initial responses can also be used to sit people of opposing views within smaller discussion groups. A further advantage is the possibility of giving anonymous answers. So if a 16 year old wants to respond that smoking is 'bad' they can see the response as part of an anonymous pie chart.

The Virtual Learning Environment (VLE)

A VLE is an application which allows learners to access, by computer, a variety of course-related learning materials and interactive systems contained within a dedicated website. Typically, a commercial VLE such as Moodle or Blackboard will have different access rights for teachers and learners, teachers having editing rights, with learners restricted to viewing rights.

On entering the VLE, a learner will usually encounter an announcement board with messages and course updates, and a series of navigation buttons which give access to the different materials contained within the VLE. These might include:

- Teaching materials such as course content and the resources used in taught sessions
- Administrative information and contacts
- Additional resources such as reading materials and web links
- Links to internal sources such as the library
- Email with other learners or groups of learners
- Discussion boards and chat rooms
- Learning packages, some of which might be interactive in nature
- Assessment activities, which may or may not be automatically marked.

Whilst originally created for distance education, now the more common function of the VLE is to supplement taught sessions, complementing face-to-face contact with electronic contact as part of a 'blended learning' approach. This can be achieved by either providing 'trigger' materials and exercises in advance of a taught session or later follow-up exercises. Some short information-based parts of the course can be delivered through the VLE by taking learners through a structured sequence of materials that might include notes, PowerPoint presentations, videos, web links, short exercises and quizzes. As with most approaches using ICT, the challenge is to make the medium interactive rather than use it to deliver information in a passive manner.

Not all learners take to the VLE immediately. They may well have to be encouraged to log on and use the site, and to regard it as part of the course delivery rather than an 'add-on'. This can be achieved by requiring learners to post a profile of themselves at the start of a course, as an icebreaker, and engage in activities such as contributing to a discussion or making use of the VLE for an assessment early in a course. Encouraging learners to take some ownership of the site, by consulting them as to what they would and would not find useful to have on it, may increase relevance and promote a more positive attitude to use.

If you do not have access to a VLE but would like to encourage your group to use electronic communication you can use an application such as wall wisher (http://www.wallwisher.com/), which acts as an online noticeboard maker on which members of the group can post comments, YouTube videos, PowerPoints, PDF documents, Excel spreadsheets, or web page links to share with each other.

Technology and communication

As well as providing visual means of communicating with learners, technology has also opened up other ways of communicating with learners. Perhaps the most common is the email which impacts daily on the lives of both teachers and learners; checking our emails has now become part of our daily routine. In an educational setting emails are now used for a number of different purposes, such as responding to course enquiries, contacting learners regarding absence or assignment submission and sending work to those who miss a class. Emails are just one of the ways in which communication between teachers and learners has been revolutionised.

Blogs can be used to keep online reflective diaries or open up discussion forums. Wikis (simple web pages that groups can edit together) can be used as part of a group project when the members of the group have limited face-to-face contact. Social networking sites can also be used to set up study or support groups, and, at an institutional level, to communicate and pass on information to learners. Skype, which allows you to see and talk to others over the Internet, can be put to good use in conducting tutorials, either individually or as small groups.

Most learners possess a mobile phone. The huge range of possible uses of the mobile phone has given rise to the concept of M-learning (learning through use of the mobile phone). This is an approach to learning which is rapidly expanding, and will become more common as each new generation of mobile phones brings further applications and increased potential to aid learning. Text messages concerning absence or class announcements are now fairly commonplace and mobile phones are often used to produce photographic evidence of work to be included in a portfolio.

The choice of e-tools for blended learning is growing rapidly. It encourages the move towards any-time, any-place learning and gives learners greater control over the pace, location and timing of their own learning.

In this chapter so far we have looked at a number of different types and uses of resources and have perhaps inspired you to make use of a wider range of those available and encouraged you to make greater use of those based on ICT. Whatever your thoughts, it is important to remember that the two important factors in getting the most out of your resources lie in:

1 The design of resources for impact and purpose
2 Making best use of resources.

Evaluating resources

You are hopefully now more confident in both designing and using resources, but as in all aspects of teaching, use and reflection on that use provides the route to improvement. The checklist below will help you in that reflective process.

Checklist for using resources

1 The resource

- Did it achieve its purpose? (create interest, focus attention, help understanding, aid memory)
- Did it use appropriate language levels for this group?
- Did it use inclusive images and examples?
- Was it 'uncluttered' and did it highlight the important learning points?
- Was it visually appealing?
- Did it give a good return for the effort spent in creating it?
- Do learners have access to the necessary technology?

2 Use of the resource

- Did I use it at the most appropriate time?
- Did I make sure learners were aware of how to use it and what its purpose was?
- Did I use it to engage learners and encourage active learning?
- Did I make sure it did not become a distraction?
- Do learners have the technical skills required?

Chapter summary

- ✓ Resources help in the processing of information by creating interest, attracting and maintaining attention, helping understanding and aiding memory.
- ✓ Resources fall into a number of different categories, ranging from prepared resources to those which are used in a more spontaneous manner.
- ✓ A consideration of design principles helps to give maximum impact to visual resources.
- ✓ Whiteboards and flip charts can be used to record spontaneous contributions as well as accommodating pre-prepared materials.
- ✓ Overhead projectors are being replaced by electronic systems such as interactive whiteboards and PowerPoint presentations, but techniques such as gradual revealing or building up of material still apply.
- ✓ The design of handouts is influenced by purpose but generally the use of 'gapped' handouts leads to a more active learning process.
- ✓ Electronic whiteboards provide an interactive resource which allows us to use any resource accessed through a computer.
- ✓ Virtual Learning Environments are now being more commonly used to complement existing forms of delivery.
- ✓ Technology provides us with a number of different resources which can be used to increase communication with learners.

 Further reading

Petty, G. (2009) *Teaching Today – A Practical Guide* (4th edn). Cheltenham: Nelson Thornes.
A highly readable book, Part 3 focuses on 'Resources for Teaching and Learning', with Chapter 35 giving a comprehensive coverage of the various resources used by teachers and Chapter 36 focusing specifically upon 'Learning with Computers'.

Hillier, Y. (2011) *Reflective Teaching in Further Education* (2nd edn). London: Continuum.
Chapter 5 'Developing Learning Resources' covers every resource imaginable, with lots of good advice on both design and use.

Clarke, A. (2011) *How To Use Technology Effectively in Post-Compulsory Education*. London: Routledge.
A very readable text which covers all the areas of technology you could possibly wish to use.

Useful websites

Joint Information Systems Committee (JISC) site which leads innovation in digital technology in education
www.jisc.ac.uk/

Make the most of PowerPoint
http://office.microsoft.com/en-gb/powerpoint/

How to use Prezi – an alternative to PowerPoint
www.prezi.com

Example prezi on assertive discipline
http://edu.prezi.com/showcase/23072/assertive-discipline/

Join the Teacher Network and gain access to a wide variety of resources
http://teachers.guardian.co.uk/

The two main interactive whiteboard makers – see their resources sections
http://www.prometheanworld.com/en-us/education/products/interactive-displays
http://smarttech.com/smartboard

How to use Wallwisher – an electronic noticeboard (free)
http://www.passyworld.com/passyPDFs/WallWisher.pdf

10

Assessing learning

Chapter overview

When you have worked through this chapter on assessing learning you will be able to:

- Identify the purposes of assessment
- Outline the stages involved in the assessment process
- Select assessment methods that are suited to the learning objectives and/or competences to be assessed
- Select assessment methods that are suited to where the learning is being assessed
- Define and recognise the importance of validity and the reliability of assessment results
- Distinguish between direct and indirect evidence
- Prepare learners to succeed in assessment
- Encourage learners to feel relaxed, ask questions and express their views
- Make an assessment decision and give constructive feedback to learners
- Complete assessment records, pass them to a relevant authority and store them securely

So far we have looked at ways of making teaching more effective; we have considered our learners, the setting of objectives, the methods that might be employed to enable learners to achieve these and the resources that might be used to support our chosen methods. If we look back to the planning cycle in Chapter 5, the other area we still need to think about is how we are going to check that the learners have achieved the learning objectives for the session.

We need now to consider the process of assessment and the methods we might use. Assessment quite simply means checking that learning has taken place. Thinking back to the journey analogy, we want to know whether we have arrived at the chosen destination.

Assessment can be defined more specifically as *all those activities and processes involved in judging performance or measuring learner achievement*.

When we start to think further about assessment, there are a number of important questions it is useful to answer.

- **Why do we assess?**
  What is the purpose of the assessments?

- **What do we assess?**
  What are the assessments actually measuring?

- **How do we assess?**
  What is the most appropriate method to use?

- **When do we assess?**
  At what point in the course/session do assessments occur?

- **Who assesses?**
  Are you the only person involved in the setting of the assessment and the decisions on the outcomes?

- **Where do we assess?**
  Does the assessment take place in the teaching or 'real-life' environment?

Assessment methods

As we progress through this chapter, we will be dealing with each of the above questions in turn. First though, it will be helpful to identify the various methods that might be used.

 Activity 10.1

Make a note of all the ways you know that can be used to check that learning has occurred.

We can ask learners, for example, to:

- Respond to questions
- Complete an exercise or test (short answer or multiple choice), either written or online
- Perform a task or skill whilst you observe
- Present evidence produced in the workplace
- Complete a project or assignment
- Write an essay
- Demonstrate to the rest of the group
- Discuss a real example
- Complete a piece of work to apply what they have learned and then report back to the rest of the group
- Take part in an aural/oral test
- Sit an exam
- Report back after discussion
- Do a quiz
- Make a presentation
- Keep a journal.

To ensure we have a common understanding of the terms above, read through the following brief descriptions.

Short answer or multiple-choice questions

These are examples of **objective testing**. These are tests with items to which there is only one correct answer. This means that the same marks will be given regardless of who does the marking.

Short answer items ask a closed question, for example: What are the five characteristics of a well-written objective?

Multiple-choice items ask the learner to select the correct answer from a number of alternative options, for example:
A well-written objective has the following characteristic:

- (a) Different people can interpret it in different ways
- (b) It is written in a specific and measurable form
- (c) It defines the overall intentions of the teacher
- (d) It is written at the completion of the teaching session
  (If you are wondering about the correct answer, think SMART.)

Both the above can be presented to learners either on paper or electronically, possibly using a Virtual Learning Environment (VLE) (see Chapter 9).

Observation

This involves watching learners whilst they complete a task or exercise as part of a teaching session, or during actual performance in the workplace, and noting down what you see.

It is often used in competence-based approaches to teaching, for example an observation of a learner completing a skill. It is normal to use a standard form or checklist to ensure consistency in observation.

Project work

This involves a substantial piece of work for which learners take responsibility. It can involve a practical task or a piece of written work involving some form of research, such as learners producing a business plan for a training company.

Essay

This is a reasonably substantial piece of written work. It asks learners to show *understanding* of the subject in which they have been taught and to present reasoned arguments. An example essay topic could be 'Discuss the advantages and disadvantages of the "whole, parts, whole" method of demonstration'.

Exams

These test learners' knowledge in a formal manner, either by written testing or completion of a practical task under controlled conditions. They are normally only applicable in teaching that leads to a recognised qualification, such as A level.

Oral and aural

These assessments test speaking and listening skills. Learners are required to listen to something and respond. They are normally used to test for understanding and are used extensively in language teaching to test for competence.

E-assessment

E-assessment provides another option for completing assessments. In the same way that e-learning refers to any form of learning that is delivered electronically, e-assessment refers to the use of information technology for any assessment-related activity. You will undoubtedly be familiar with this approach, as most initial assessments of numeracy and literacy take this form.

E-assessment is a rapidly developing area and can take a number of different forms; it lends itself most readily to replicating current paper testing. The candidate answers the questions electronically, which means that the test can also be marked electronically as well as manually. It does mean that questions have to be closed in nature, but leads to high degrees of reliability (see later in this chapter).

The electronic medium provides a number of advantages over the paper-based approach. The use of images, sound and video clips in the test offers extra possibilities, and testing can simulate 'real-life' situations. Drag and drop options are also available.

Testing can be made more individual by using branching programmes whereby the answers given determine a personalised route through the test itself. If candidates are progressing well they can be directed to more difficult questions, whereas those who are doing less well can be tested at a simpler and more appropriate level. E-assessment does require some ICT skills of the learner. If the learners do not have the appropriate level of Functional Skills this may raise problems with validity (see later in this chapter), particularly if the test is time-bound.

Purposes of assessment

We have now identified a variety of assessment methods we can use with learners. To help us to choose appropriate assessment methods, we first need to consider the specific purpose of any assessment. We need to know **why** we are assessing in order to decide how best to go about it.

You will probably have been involved in various types of assessment as a learner yourself. Draw on this experience in completing the following activity.

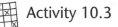

Activity 10.2

Identify the **purpose** of each of the assessments below. It may help you to think about how the method was of benefit to the teacher and/or the learner.

- Driving test
- Short informal quiz during a session
- Online language testing prior to starting a course
- Observation of a receptionist greeting visitors

There are many different reasons for engaging in assessment. They can be considered as falling into two main groups:

1 Assessment *of* learning. This is the type of assessment which is related to accountability. Governments (through inspection processes) wish to monitor standards; governors, parents and others wish to monitor progress. Employers (through certification) want to know about competence. Learners wish to have certification to provide recognition of the level they have achieved.
2 Assessment *for* learning. The purpose of this type of assessment is to support teaching and learning. Reasonably detailed feedback is available to teachers and learners which can be used to modify teaching and learning to make it more effective.

Activity 10.3

Into which of the above groups does each of your examples from Activity 10.2 fit?

The more specific reasons for assessing learners include:

☑ Check learning objectives have been achieved.
☑ Monitor learner's progress.
☑ Correct errors in performance.
☑ Diagnose particular areas of concern.
☑ Predict whether learners can cope with the demands or level of programme applied for.
☑ Provide motivation through demonstrating achievement.
☑ Enable learners to identify their own strengths.
☑ Provide feedback to learners.
☑ Provide information to improve teaching/training and learning.
☑ Inform the planning of future sessions.
☑ Select individuals for further teaching or employment.
☑ Recognise achievement by awarding certification.

In considering our choice of assessment methods we need to be clear about what the purpose of the assessment is. For some of these purposes assessment needs to be **formal**. In other instances it can be **informal**. Formal assessment, as the name implies, will generally involve assessment results being formally recorded. Learners will know they are being assessed.

Suppose, however, that we set learners a task to perform. In their minds, it is an exercise that will help their learning, or, particularly in the case of a skill, they may regard it as practice to refine their technique. Whilst they are engaged in the exercise, we can observe carefully to see if they are doing it correctly or are making mistakes. Although they do not regard this as a test, we are nonetheless assessing them, but the whole process is much less threatening. To distinguish this type of assessment from the more formal methods we call it informal assessment, the crucial difference being that learners are not aware that they are being assessed.

Both formal and informal assessments have their place in the teaching we do. Between them, they can achieve all of the purposes previously mentioned. How do you use these different forms of assessment in your own working context?

Activity 10.4

When do your learners undergo formal assessment?

When do your learners undergo informal assessment?

What we assess has to be placed within a context of purpose. Having considered *why* we assess, the time has now come to think about *what* it is we are assessing and *how* we will go about it.

Selecting appropriate methods

When we looked at planning a teaching session we decided the first step was to specify what we wanted our learners to learn. To do this we wrote learning objectives, detailing the learning that would be achieved. If they are SMART objectives then they will be written in a specific and measurable way that will give us clues about how to assess them.

Look at the following two objectives:

At the end of the session each learner will be able to:

1 Ride a bicycle safely in a straight line, unaided, for a distance of 100 metres
2 Understand how to mend a puncture in a bicycle tyre.

Activity 10.5

How would you assess each of the above objectives?

You will undoubtedly have found it more straightforward to arrive at an assessment method for the first objective. You will recognise that the first is a SMART objective and contains an action verb that gives a clear indication of the precise learning that will occur.

Consider this learning objective:

At the end of the session, each learner will be able to describe the functions of the heart.

The verb in the learning objective 'describe' gives us a clue about how this could be assessed; we would need to set up conditions in which learners could 'describe'. This description could be oral or written and our choice would depend on our situation. This precise statement of learning provides us with a signpost to the most appropriate assessment method.

If the objective is imprecise, as in example 2 above, it is much more difficult to assess. We have to reword the objective, in our heads, into a SMART form to reach an assessment decision.

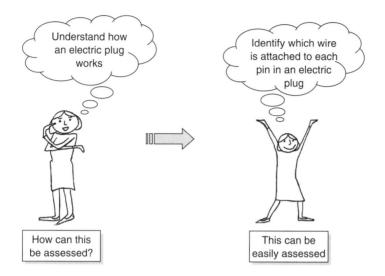

So, SMART objectives are essential to the assessment process. This in itself, however, is not sufficient; there are additional considerations to take into account.

Let us look again at a previous objective:

> *At the end of the session each learner will be able to ride a bicycle safely in a straight line, unaided, for a distance of 100 metres.*

Would you use a written test on bicycle riding to assess whether or not this objective had been achieved? Would this type of assessment actually measure what you intend it to measure – the ability to ride a bike unaided for 100 metres?

A written test on bicycle riding might allow you to test whether your learner had grasped the **knowledge** needed to ride a bicycle, but you would not know whether they could actually **ride** the bicycle for 100 metres unaided. To find this out we would have to observe learners actually riding a bike and make some judgement on how successfully they were able to do this.

 ## Activity 10.6

Consider how you would assess the following objective in a way that measures what you intend to measure.

At the end of the session, each learner will be able to order three dishes in Mandarin in a Chinese restaurant.

In your choice of assessment you would expect an opportunity for the learner to show not only a knowledge of the language but also some oral competence. Remember, if your objective is knowledge based your assessment should check knowledge, if your objective is skill based your assessment should check skills.

Validity and reliability

The last examples illustrate one of two important qualities that all assessments must possess. We must ensure that the assessment method we choose tests the actual ability we wish it to test. In the language of assessment this is known as validity.

In order to produce VALID results, an assessment procedure must actually measure what we intend it to measure.

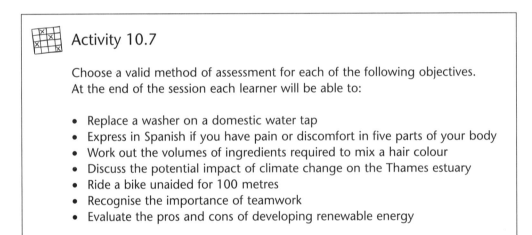

Activity 10.7

Choose a valid method of assessment for each of the following objectives. At the end of the session each learner will be able to:

- Replace a washer on a domestic water tap
- Express in Spanish if you have pain or discomfort in five parts of your body
- Work out the volumes of ingredients required to mix a hair colour
- Discuss the potential impact of climate change on the Thames estuary
- Ride a bike unaided for 100 metres
- Recognise the importance of teamwork
- Evaluate the pros and cons of developing renewable energy

Having thought about what it is we want to assess and identified a method that will give us valid results, we proceed with the assessment. The next stage involves making some judgement on what has been produced. The judgement we reach should give an accurate reflection of a person's ability. Quite often this is not the case as the final decision can be influenced by a number of factors.

Consider the example we have previously used:

At the end of the session each learner will be able to ride a bicycle safely in a straight line, unaided, for a distance of 100 metres.

We have agreed that in order to assess this learning we would observe the learner riding a bicycle for a distance of 100 metres. It would appear easy to make a judgement on this, but all sorts of variables may come into play and influence the judgement we reach. A further complication arises when a number of different people undertake the same assessment, possibly at the same time.

 Activity 10.8

What do you think might influence the outcomes of the bicycle riding assessment?

There are a number of factors that could possibly influence the results of the assessment and they fall broadly under three categories: factors to do with the learners, external factors and factors to do with the assessor.

- **The learner**: Not feeling well, nervous about test, inappropriate frame of mind, unsure what is expected of them
- **External factors**: Wrong size of bicycle, different equipment from one practised on, defective equipment, bad weather conditions, road surface
- **The assessor**: Likes or dislikes the candidate, different assessors, concentration varies according to number of candidates, assessor not feeling well.

Looking at the factors above it is evident that there are some factors over which we have some control and others over which we have none. For example, we cannot influence the health of either candidate or assessor, but we can ensure that every candidate has appropriate equipment of the same standard. These issues relate to the second key point in assessment – not only should results be valid, they should also be reliable.

> *The results of assessment can be considered RELIABLE if the same candidate would achieve the same result for the assessment if it were taken on another occasion or with another assessor.*

How can we ensure results that are reliable? Results should not be influenced by the occasion on which the learner takes the assessment or by our perceptions or opinions when we carry out the assessment. In other words, there must be **consistency** in the administration of the assessment procedure.

With the best intentions in the world, it is difficult, if not impossible, to achieve absolute consistency. We can, however, be more consistent by adopting a number of strategies.

In our bicycle example, our results would be more reliable if the assessor had measured the candidate's performance against a set of specific criteria. We could devise a checklist that states exactly what is required and the learner's performance can be measured against this. The more detailed and specific the checklist, the more reliable the results of our assessment will be.

Within a teaching context, all assessment decisions should be based on clear, well-defined criteria. If the assessment criteria are clear when the work is set, deciding whether a learner has met the criteria should be straightforward. More importantly, clear criteria help us to avoid bias – factors that affect the judgements made by the person doing the assessing. Bias will decrease the reliability of the assessment results. As well as helping to avoid bias in assessment decisions, knowledge of criteria will also help learners to perform better, as they will be clear as to how success will be judged.

Bias can arise in many different ways and includes anything that influences the decisions at which we arrive. It generally occurs as an unintended consequence of the actions we take within the assessment process; so we are not even aware that what we are doing will lead to bias in our judgements.

 Activity 10.9

What do you think might introduce bias into the assessment process?

You may have considered the assessor being influenced by factors such as:

- The assessor's frame of mind
- The personality of the learner
- The presentation rather than the content of the work to be assessed
- The conditions under which the assessment is taking place
- Whether the learner is the first or the last to be assessed. It is likely that earlier assessments will be conducted in a different manner to later assessments
- The assessor's stereotype of the most likely candidate to succeed. This could be related to factors such as gender, age and background that we discussed in Chapter 6
- The assessor's previous experiences of the candidate. If a candidate has performed well on a previous occasion the assessor will be expecting a good performance and may judge it more favourably. The opposite can also happen. If the result is a positive bias, it is known as the 'halo' effect, whereas negative bias represents the 'horns' effect.

When do we assess?

As we saw earlier, assessment has a wide range of purposes. The purpose of an assessment will have a bearing not only on how we assess, but also when we assess. We have already looked at initial assessment in Chapter 6; now we turn our attention to our assessment of learners once they are 'on programme'.

1   At the **beginning** of a teaching session we may ask the learners questions to find out how much they know about the subject we are about to teach. This allows us to draw on experience in the group to pitch the teaching session at the appropriate level for the learners and build upon their existing level of knowledge and skills. We could achieve this by a short written test or a quiz. Whatever the method we use, we would call this type of assessment **diagnostic**. Its purpose is to establish the presence or absence of existing knowledge and skills in addition to any knowledge we have already gained.

2   As the session progresses we continue to assess, typically by asking questions and observing learners practising what they have learned. At this stage our purpose is to check learners' progress. This helps us, as teachers, to gauge the extent of learning and to ensure the pace of learning is appropriate. For the learners it provides feedback to help them to correct mistakes, to improve upon technique and to gain some idea of the progress they are making. This type of assessment can take place at any time or times **during** the teaching session. As it helps to 'shape' the session it is termed **formative** assessment.

3   At the **end** of the teaching session, we wish to make a judgement on whether the objectives for that particular session have been achieved. Again, the methods we use to do this are varied and may be formal or informal. What we seek to find out is the 'sum' total of the knowledge or skills that the learners have acquired at that particular time. This type of assessment is therefore known as **summative**.

Activity 10.10

Thinking of assessments you might ask your learners to undertake, identify an example for each of the three purposes above: diagnostic, formative or summative.

It is important that both teachers/assessors and learners know how successful learning has been at all stages of teaching. The particular aspect of that success we wish to measure determines **when** – at what stage in teaching – we assess. In the above activity you selected specific assessment methods for specific purposes in your own teaching context. The information box below shows the relationship between the purpose and timing of assessment. This will influence your choice of method.

When?	Why?	Type of assessment
Beginning	To establish existing knowledge, experience or skills	Diagnostic
During	To inform both teacher and learner of progress	Formative
End	To check objectives have been achieved	Summative

Who assesses?

So far we have talked about assessment as if it is always the teacher or assessor who administers it. While this is likely to be the case most of the time, it is possible for assessment to take place without either being present. It is often difficult for the teacher to see all of the learners, spend time with individuals and give sufficient feedback. The solution to this may be to involve learners themselves in the process of assessment. This can be achieved by a variety of methods, particularly e-assessment, which can take place outside of formal teaching time, and so has the added advantage of providing an additional learning opportunity (see http:// teachers.guardian.co.uk/ for examples of e-assessment).

Learners can take part in the assessment process by assessing themselves, known as **self assessment**, or by assessing each other, known as **peer assessment**. But how can they do this if they are only just learning a procedure themselves? We can provide a checklist that lists all the stages in the procedure in the correct order. Learners can refer to the checklist in order to check their own performance (self assessment) or alternatively they may work in pairs or small groups to check each other's performance and give feedback (peer assessment). Learners could, for instance, work in a group of three:

- Learner 1 demonstrates the skill in question
- Learner 2 is used if necessary as a subject
- Learner 3 checks Learner 1's performance against the checklist
- All three learners discuss the performance of Learner 1
- The exercise can be repeated with each learner in a different role.

This method can also lead to additional learning, as all learners will benefit from the discussion of performance. We can go around the small groups making our own observations and comments whilst this is happening. Although not all areas of assessment lend themselves easily to this approach it has considerable potential.

Activity 10.11

Consider your own teaching/learning – can you identify any examples when you have experienced or could have used self or peer assessment?

Designing assessments

If you are devising your own assessments you will need to consider a variety of factors we have already discussed. The checklist below will help you in designing your method of assessment and introduces some new terms.

Assessment checklist

Is the method:

☑ *Valid*
It should assess what you really want to measure.

☑ *Reliable*
Criteria and marking schemes should be clear, so that different tutors should arrive at the same result.

☑ *Transparent*
Is it clear what is being assessed and how judgements are being made?

☑ *Fair*
Learners should have an equal chance to succeed, even if their experiences are not identical. Literacy, numeracy, ICT, bilingualism or cultural aspects should be taken into account. Learners should also consider the assessment fair.

☑ *Equitable*
It should not disadvantage any learner or group. Using a range of assessment methods will help.

☑ *Formative*
It should enable the learner to review progress and plan further learning.

☑ *Timely*
It should give early opportunities for rehearsal and feedback.

☑ *Authentic*
You need to be certain that it is the learner's own work that you are assessing.

Preparing learners to succeed in assessment

Whichever assessment method we choose, we want learners to perform in a manner that gives an accurate reflection of their ability. It is more likely this will happen if we prepare them to succeed. This preparation involves consideration of:

- The physical and social environment in which the assessment will take place
- The learners, ensuring they are fully aware of what to expect in an assessment and what is expected of them.

The emphasis within each of these will differ depending on whether the assessment is internally or externally administered.

In the activity below you are asked how you would consider these two aspects in practice. In your consideration of an appropriate environment for assessment you may wish to refer back to ideas about creating the right environment in Chapter 2.

Activity 10.12

What do you consider an appropriate environment for assessment would include?

What do you think learners need to know prior to assessment?

In terms of the environment you may have identified some of the following:

- Putting learners at ease by using first names
- Using open body language
- Arranging suitable room layout
- Checking sufficient resources are available
- Ensuring there are no unnecessary barriers to assessment.

Your 'need to know' list may include:

- What is the purpose of the assessment?
- When will the assessment take place?
- How long will the assessment be?
- Which assessment methods will be used?
- What equipment and books will be allowed?
- What will marks be awarded for?
- How will results be handled and fed back to the group?

Learners will not feel adequately prepared for assessment unless they are clear about such information. Perhaps more importantly, learners are more likely to perform to their potential if we help them to understand the assessment and why it is needed. This involves making the assessment criteria clear, and so helping learners to recognise exactly what it is that they need to do in order to succeed.

We can help learners to feel more confident about the assessment process if we provide opportunities for them to practise beforehand in a safe environment, and give feedback on their techniques. Encouraging learners to feel relaxed and able to ask questions can also help them to feel confident and help them to perform better. This applies particularly to assessments we administer ourselves. In a formal examination setting, it is essential to adhere to regulations and a more formal code of conduct. We can also help learners to manage their time effectively and encourage them to help each other prepare for assessment. If learners feel confident about what is required of them, they will have a higher chance of success in demonstrating their achievements.

Constructive feedback

Once an assessment decision has been reached, we can consider how decisions can be conveyed to learners in a manner that will not only inform them of the outcome but will also help them learn from the experience of the assessment. To give effective feedback we should include a consideration of:

- Which criteria have been achieved
- Which criteria have not been achieved and why
- What the learner needs to do to become successful.

A key consideration when giving feedback is that it should be targeted to enhance learning. It should occur as soon after the assessment as possible, concentrating on what the learner should do to improve rather than being heavily judgemental. We have already looked at a model identifying the stages in giving feedback in Chapter 8. The sequence and content of feedback is not the only consideration; we need to think carefully about *how* to give feedback constructively so that learners can see its value.

Activity 10.13

Reflect on occasions when you received or gave feedback.

What did you consider were the negative aspects of feedback?

What made feedback a positive experience?

The purpose of feedback is to help learners improve what they are doing. It follows that feedback has to be useful and given in a manner that supports the learner. The following guidelines may help you:

Giving constructive feedback:

- ☑ Keep the time short between performance and feedback; where possible give immediate feedback.
- ☑ Take account of the feelings of learners.
- ☑ Encourage learners to evaluate themselves. Help learners to identify what went well; aim for a dialogue.
- ☑ Demonstrate active listening.
- ☑ Balance negative and positive comments. Begin by thanking the learner for the work; start and end on a positive note.
- ☑ Relate your feedback to the criteria set.
- ☑ Give only two or three main points of advice; learners can soon reach information overload.
- ☑ Distinguish between different skills, for instance the learner may have lots of good ideas, but poor organisation.
- ☑ Offer help and make further suggestions. Concentrate on how the learner can improve in the future.
- ☑ Summarise and agree an action plan.

If your feedback is written:

- ☑ Try to do more than give ticks; comments are more motivating.
- ☑ Avoid putting crosses and using too much red pen.
- ☑ Explain to learners what they have to do to improve.
- ☑ Make your writing legible.

Record keeping

Assessment is one of the most important tasks of a teacher. We must not forget to keep accurate and confidential records of this aspect of our work. There are a number of reasons for this which could be thought of as 'internal' and 'external'.

In an 'internal' sense, we need to monitor learners' progress. Any course or programme invariably contains a number of different assessment activities and the results of these need to be recorded on some form of tracking sheet. This allows us to see at a glance the progress (or lack of it) that each learner is making, and informs tutorials, reviews and Individual Learning Plans. Where we see areas of weakness common to all learners it is a signal to us to ensure that particular topic or area is consolidated and to consider how it was taught in the first instance. These records will be used internally and this relates to our earlier discussion of assessment for learning.

There are a number of 'external' parties who also have an interest in the achievement of learners. Parents or employers, for instance, may well want to know of progress;

backing up comments with the evidence of actual marks creates a much more credible and professional impression. External verifiers and awarding bodies will require a complete audit trail of learner achievement before final certification or accreditation can be given and the only effective and reliable way to achieve this is by continuous and accurate record keeping. Records required externally are needed, as we described earlier, for assessment *of* learning.

An important aspect of quality assurance in Further Education relates to retention of learners and their achievements. Records of both are required to calculate achievement and success rates that will inform future provision and resourcing. It is evident, then, that the recording of the results of assessment is a vital part of the teacher's role and you should bear the following in mind:

- **Be meticulous:** Record marks accurately and immediately
- **Be systematic:** File all records of assessment in a secure, agreed place
- **Be reliable:** Pass records promptly on to the appropriate authority
- **Use technology:** Produce **assessment records** and figures using IT.

Being well organised in your assessment record keeping makes you more efficient and makes others more confident of your professionalism.

Chapter summary

The main points covered in this chapter are:

✓ Assessment can have a number of different purposes. Assessment methods should fulfil their intended purpose.
✓ Assessments can be formal or informal, and in the case of the latter, the learner may not be aware that learning is being checked.
✓ All assessment methods should produce results that are valid (measure what they intend to measure) and reliable (show consistency).
✓ Assessment can take place at the beginning (diagnostic), during (formative) or at the end (summative) of an episode of learning.
✓ E-assessment reduces paperwork, allows any-time access and immediate feedback.
✓ With sufficient guidance, learners can assess their own work (self assessment) or the work of other learners (peer assessment).

 **Further reading**

Black, P., Harrison, C., Lee, C., Marshall, B. and Wiliam, D. (2003) *Assessment for Learning: Putting it into Practice*. Maidenhead: Open University Press.
Reviews the principles underlying assessment for learning and how to put these into practice.

Ecclestone, K. (2005) *Understanding Assessment and Qualifications in Post-Compulsory Education and Training* (2nd edn). Leicester: NIACE.
This provides a deeper look at assessment and assessment issues. Chapter 1 examines purpose and types of assessment, while Chapter 2 looks at the characteristics of assessment.

Huddleston, P. and Unwin, L. (2002) *Teaching and Learning in Further Education* (2nd edn). London: Routledge Falmer.
Chapter 6 on assessment and recording achievement looks at formative and summative approaches to assessment before giving a comprehensive overview of different methods of assessment.

Irons, A. (2008) *Enhancing Learning through Formative Assessment and Feedback*. London: Routledge.
If you want a more in-depth treatment of formative assessment, this book will provide it. It also offers comprehensive coverage of giving feedback. Written for those who work in Higher Education, it provides a challenging but stimulating read.

Tummons, J. (2011) *Assessing Learning in the Lifelong Learning Sector* (2nd edn). Exeter: Learning Matters.
Chapter 7 gives sound advice and examples of methods of recording the results of assessment as well as the rationale behind this activity.

Useful websites

Top ten tips on assessment for learning
http://www.kent.ac.uk/uelt/ced/themes/assessment/pdf_files/TTTasmforlearning.pdf

Hot potatoes – a free site that lets you create online assessments
http://hotpot.uvic.ca/

A more sophisticated e-learning site, but sophistication comes at a price
www.knowledgepresenter.com/assets/home.htm

11

Competence-based assessment

Chapter overview

When you have worked through this chapter on assessing learning you will be able to:

■ Define competence-based assessment
■ Describe the roles of those involved in vocational assessment
■ Develop a plan for a competence-based assessment
■ Outline the quality assurance process for vocational programmes

Assessing competence

Many of us in the lifelong learning sector are involved in vocational qualifications (VQs) which relate to specific occupational roles. We ensure learners are able to use what they have learned in vocational contexts and are competent at the level required by an employer. Others of you could be supporting learners to gain competence-based qualifications which may not be directly related to employment.

In this book competence is defined as:

The ability of an individual to demonstrate the capacity to use the knowledge, skills and appropriate attitudes required in order to carry out a work-related role, to the current national standard within the relevant occupational area.

Earlier in the chapter we looked at the principles and practice of assessment which apply in any teaching context, but we will now focus on competence-based assessment, and also relate these principles and practice to the more specific vocational setting. This section is intended to help you develop and/or reflect on your skills as an assessor of competence.

Structure of vocational qualifications

Within a given vocational area, the relevant Sector Skills Council creates a set of occupational standards which define the competences required to perform specific job roles. Awarding Bodies such as Edexcel, then develop and offer qualifications which meet these occupational standards and also fit within the Qualifications and Credit Framework (QCF).

The QCF is the national qualification structure which subdivides learning into units at different levels of difficulty from 1 to 8.

The units attract credit points related to the quantity of learning involved. These units can be combined to make qualifications of different credit size:

Award	1–12 credits
Certificate	13–36 credits
Diploma	37+ credits

You are currently interested in the PTLLS Award (12 credits) but may then be keen to develop further with a higher qualification in Lifelong Learning. Similarly, you may be interested in achieving a qualification as a vocational assessor and combining this with other units in Learning and Development to achieve a Level 3 or Level 4 Certificate or Diploma in Learning and Development.

The title of a qualification, therefore, provides three pieces of information – level, subject and type of qualification related to credit size.

Some qualifications are titled NVQs (National Vocational Qualifications), such as NVQ Level 3 Certificate in Health and Social Care.

Activity 11.1

Do you know which awards, certificates or diplomas are available in your specialist area? Check this out on the Register of regulated qualification http://register.ofqual.gov.uk/

The Unit 'Facilitate learning and development in groups' appears on the QCF. It is a Level 3 unit with a credit value of 6. This is part of the Certificate and Diploma in Learning and Development. It is also currently an alternative unit for the PTLLS Award, providing six of the 12 credits required.

The Unit describes an aspect of a vocational role. Each unit is subdivided into elements and/or learning outcomes. In the unit 'Facilitate learning and development in groups' there are four learning outcomes; one of these is:

Learning Outcome 4: Be able to assist individual learners in reflecting on their learning and/or development.

Each outcome contains assessment criteria specifying what is required for competent performance – for example, in the case of Learning Outcome 4:

4.1 Explain benefits of self-evaluation to individuals.
4.2 Review individual responses to one-to-one learning and/or development.
4.3 Assist individual learners to identify their future learning and/or development needs.

It is against these criteria that candidates are judged to be competent.

This credit and unit-based approach adopted in the QCF can result in greater flexibility for learners, both in the way in which they can select units and in the pace at which they can accumulate these. For adult learners this can mean a qualification that meets their needs more precisely and fits with the availability of their time. It also means that they can gain formal recognition for smaller amounts of learning.

Roles in vocational assessment

In Chapter 1 we discussed the role of the teacher in the lifelong learning sector and acknowledged the multiple roles which this involves. Competence-based assessment involves a candidate, an assessor, an internal verifier, an external verifier. Any or all of these roles could be part of your role set. We shall look at who these are and what part each plays in the assessment process.

If you are putting yourself forward for the PTLLS Award then you are a candidate for this award. The person(s) approved by the Awarding Body as competent to make judgements about the candidate are called assessors. An assessor has to be able to show competence in their own vocational or specialist area and be qualified as an assessor. The quality of their judgements will be assured by an Internal Verifier (IV), appointed by your Centre, and the Awarding Body in turn will recruit External or Standards Verifiers (EVs or SVs) to confirm the work of the IV and to ensure that the standards are being met and processes duly observed. Any or all of these roles could be part of your role set, identified in Chapter 1.

Stages in competence-based assessment

Competence-based assessment follows the four stages outlined below. We will look at each of these stages in turn.

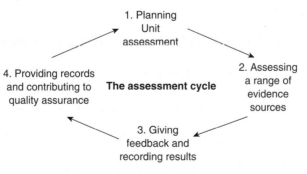

Stage 1 – Planning and preparing for assessment

Both the assessor and the candidate need to plan and prepare carefully to ensure that any assessment is both efficient and effective. It may take a while for a candidate to relate the units, competences and performance criteria to their occupational context. You have a role to ensure all candidates are thoroughly familiar with the assessment requirements well in advance of any assessment taking place.

Communication needs to take place between the assessor and the candidate to:

- Develop an overall unit assessment plan
- Achieve clarity about which competencies need to be assessed
- Agree the best circumstances for these to be demonstrated
- Consider any other competences which could be observed, for example Health and Safety
- Agree dates, times and venues which give the optimum opportunity and are mutually convenient.

This conversation may happen during a group tutorial, an individual meeting, a telephone conversation, by Skype or email. The important end result is clarity.

Where do we assess?

Not all assessments can best take place in the teaching environment. Often, as for instance in NVQs, assessment is carried out in the learner's workplace. There are advantages and disadvantages if this is the case, and these will need to be considered carefully. The choice of environment in which the assessment takes place will be influenced by what is to be assessed and how it is to be assessed.

Activity 11.2

What do you think are the advantages of assessing in the workplace?

What do you think are the limitations of assessing in the workplace?

Some of the possible advantages you may have considered are:

- Adequate equipment is available with which the learner is familiar
- The setting is realistic; to demonstrate some skills learners need to be working in real-life situations
- The learner does not waste time travelling to an assessment centre.

Whilst the possible limitations include:

- Finding an appropriate place from which to observe
- Disrupting the work procedures
- Difficult to concentrate
- Distraction from other employees.

Whether the most appropriate location for the assessment is the workplace or the teaching environment, we find that learners perform better if they are prepared for success.

Once you have reached decisions with your candidate you will be able to draw up an assessment plan for a specific occasion, including details such as:

- What competences and criteria will be assessed?
- When will it take place – date and time?
- Where will the assessment take place?
- What resources will be needed?
- If it involves an observation, what arrangements need to be made with the employer or possibly clients?
- How will the assessment decision be recorded? What documentation will be required? What will the candidate receive?
- When and how will feedback be given?

Stage 2 – Assessing a range of evidence sources

Candidates need to be able to provide evidence of their competence. Where possible this will be provided by direct evidence from performance in the workplace assessed by an assessor. Indirect evidence can be generated from a number of sources.

 Activity 11.3

Consider the Unit 'Facilitate learning and development in groups', referred to earlier. What evidence could a candidate provide to show they are competent to:

4.1 Explain benefits of self-evaluation to individuals.

4.3 Assist individual learners to identify their future learning and/or development needs.

As we saw earlier when discussing the writing of learning objectives, the clue to assessment lies in the verb, in this case 'explain' or 'assist'. The evidence requirements for this Unit stipulate that evidence for Learning Outcome 4 must come from performance in the work environment and examining products of work ('direct evidence'). Supplementary evidence ('indirect' evidence) may be gathered by questioning, discussion and use of others (witness statements).

Observation provides the main source of evidence for vocational competence. It is usual for an assessor to record the competences observed on a checklist and to have thought through how the underpinning knowledge will be checked. We cannot assume that a candidate who can perform competently has the underpinning knowledge. It is possible for candidates to imitate colleagues and have no idea why they are doing what they are! Audio and video recordings are sometimes submitted as an alternative to live observation.

Questioning (see Chapter 8) is the main method used to check underpinning knowledge and understanding. It is also used to assess whether candidates understand how they might need to adapt their performance to fit other vocational situations that they could encounter, particularly if their job role is narrow or organisational requirements less stringent. Written tests, projects and professional discussions provide alternatives to questioning.

It may be the case that a candidate has previously achieved a qualification that overlaps with this unit. Provided the original certificate can be produced and is deemed current (up to date with present practice) then recognition of prior learning (RPL)/ accreditation of prior learning (APL) may take place, subject to Awarding Body guidance.

In all assessment procedures, whatever method is used, the evidence collected should be: valid, reliable, authentic and current.

Candidates will normally collect their evidence in a portfolio. Increasingly these are e-portfolios, which Clarke (2011: 105) defines as 'collections of digital evidence that show the learners' skills, knowledge and understanding'. Portfolios need to be organised in a logical and systematic way. The assessor (and subsequently possibly an internal or external verifier) needs to be able to quickly gain an overview of its contents and be able to locate evidence with ease. E-portfolios have the advantage of being able to capture a wider range of evidence, including videos and digital images.

Stage 3 – Giving feedback and recording results
Ollin and Tucker (2008: 49) consider 'The skill of giving constructive and helpful feedback is at the heart of successful assessment'. We have highlighted the main features of effective feedback in the previous chapter.

Candidates need to be clear about precisely which competences they have achieved, which they have not achieved and what they need to do to meet the criteria for competence. So, a key feature of effective feedback is always to highlight areas for consolidation, improvement and development, and agree these with the candidate. The final stage of feedback should be to agree an action plan and assessment plan for the next step.

Assessors need to be clear at all times about how much candidates have achieved; this is the purpose of a tracking document.

Stage 4 – Providing records and contributing to quality assurance

Earlier in this chapter we noted that the recording of the results of assessment is a vital part of the teacher's role. The following rules equally apply to any vocational assessments.

- **Be meticulous:** Record assessment outcomes/competences accurately and immediately
- **Be systematic:** File all records of assessment in a secure, agreed place
- **Be reliable:** Use documentation approved by the Awarding Body and pass records promptly on to the appropriate authority
- **Use technology:** Produce assessment records and figures using IT.

Your records will be sampled and checked by both your IV and the Awarding Body EV or SV as part of the quality assurance procedures for the programme. The quality assurance procedure will also outline a process to be followed in the event of a dispute related to assessment judgements. You will be able to benefit from advice, support and guidance, both internally and externally.

Improving your assessor skills

It is vital that you learn from your experience of assessing if you are to progress.

We will discuss self evaluation in the next chapter. The assessment experience provides additional opportunities for evaluation through discussion with your learners/candidates, colleagues/fellow assessors and internal verifier.

To be a qualified vocational assessor you will need sufficient occupational knowledge and experience at or above the Unit being assessed and possess the relevant assessor qualifications. Hopefully this chapter will enable you to work towards these awards if required.

Checklist for competence-based assessment

> ☑ Are the assessment criteria clear to the candidate?
> ☑ Have I ensured that the candidate is at ease?
> ☑ Have I considered Functional Skills?
> ☑ Is the assessment plan clear?
> ☑ Can the competence really be demonstrated in the time allocated?
> ☑ Has the candidate ensured that the necessary resources are available?
> ☑ Have we agreed where and how feedback will be given?
> ☑ Do I have the paperwork to record decisions?
> ☑ Have I considered where I will position myself during the assessment?

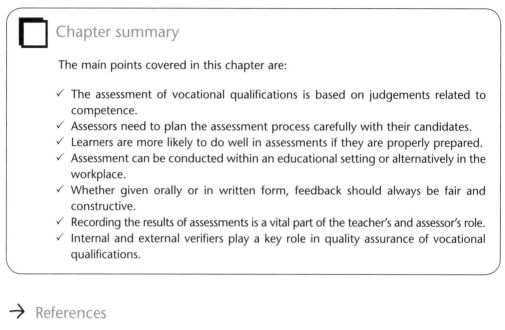

Chapter summary

The main points covered in this chapter are:

- ✓ The assessment of vocational qualifications is based on judgements related to competence.
- ✓ Assessors need to plan the assessment process carefully with their candidates.
- ✓ Learners are more likely to do well in assessments if they are properly prepared.
- ✓ Assessment can be conducted within an educational setting or alternatively in the workplace.
- ✓ Whether given orally or in written form, feedback should always be fair and constructive.
- ✓ Recording the results of assessments is a vital part of the teacher's and assessor's role.
- ✓ Internal and external verifiers play a key role in quality assurance of vocational qualifications.

→ References

Clarke, A. (2011) *How to Use Technology Effectively in Post Compulsory Education*. London: Routledge.

Ollin, R. and Tucker, J. (2008) *The NVQ Assessor and Verifier & Candidate Handbook* (4th edn). London: Kogan Page.

 Useful websites

Register of regulated qualification
http://register.ofqual.gov.uk/

An interesting critique of competence-based assessment from Alison Wolf
http://www.heacademy.ac.uk/assets/documents/resources/heca/heca_cl25.pdf

Further reading

Fletcher, S. (2000) *Competence-Based Assessment Techniques* (2nd edn). London: Kogan Page.
This book provides a comprehensive overview of the key principles, methods, implications and benefits of competence-based approaches. It is divided into two parts. Part One examines the purpose and use of the different competence-based systems while Part Two concentrates on practical application, outlining the stages in the assessment process and looking at a range of different approaches to assessment.

Wolf, A. (1995) *Competence-Based Assessment*. Buckingham: Open University Press.
If you are looking for something less practical and more theoretical, this is the book for you. It provides the background to the emergence of the competence-based movement as well as a more theoretical analysis of its underlying assumptions and relationship to criterion-referenced approaches.

12

Supporting Functional Skills development

Chapter overview

When you have worked through this chapter on Functional Skills you will be able to:

- Define Functional Skills
- Recognise the need to support the development of learners' Functional Skills
- Map Functional Skills needed by learners in your subject
- Identify strategies you can use to embed Functional Skills in everyday teaching
- Provide opportunities for learners to practise their English, Maths and ICT skills
- Identify institutional or other support for Functional Skills development
- Review your own Functional Skills and plan to develop as required

What are Functional Skills?

In Chapter 8 you considered how to support learners in acquiring the knowledge, skills and attitudes related to your subject specialism. But there are other skills learners need in order to be successful in their learning.

You may have heard statements such as:

'5 million adults in the UK cannot read the Yellow Pages'.

'8 million adults cannot work out the correct amount of medicine to give a child from the label on a packet'.

These adults do not have the skills to function and progress in everyday life and work; 5 million lack functional literacy; 8 million lack functional numeracy (Department for Business, Innovation and Skills, 2011: 4). Whilst this is indeed a problem for those individuals, it is also a major problem for the government, as it is estimated that such low skills are a significant cost to the UK economy.

The government launched a Skills for Life strategy in 2000 to improve adults' basic skills. Over a decade later, the current government remains committed to removing barriers to employment which may be caused by a lack of Functional Skills.

We need to be aware that this is an area where terminology is changing rapidly. Literacy and numeracy are sometimes used interchangeably with English and Maths and previous descriptors such as basic skills and key skills continue to be used after Key Skills qualifications have been withdrawn. The term Functional Skills, however, is currently widely used to encompass all of the above.

We can define 'Functional Skills' as *the fundamental, applied skills in English, Mathematics, and Information and Communication Technology (ICT) that provide an individual with the essential knowledge, skills and understanding to enable them to operate confidently, effectively and independently in life, education and work*.

Functional Skills qualifications in English assess:

- Speaking, listening and communication
- Reading
- Writing

Functional Skills qualifications in Mathematics assess:

- Representing – understanding and using mathematical information/ selecting the mathematics and information to model a situation
- Analysing, processing and using mathematics
- Interpreting and communicating the results of analysis

Functional Skills qualifications in Information and Communications Technology (ICT) assess:

- Use of ICT systems
- Finding and selecting information
- Developing, presenting and communicating information

Functional Skills qualifications in English, Maths and ICT are currently available at Entry 1, Entry 2, Entry 3, Level 1 and Level 2.

You may well be thinking, 'What does all this have to do with me as a teacher of plastering?' (or whatever your particular specialism is). Pose yourself the questions asked in the illustration below.

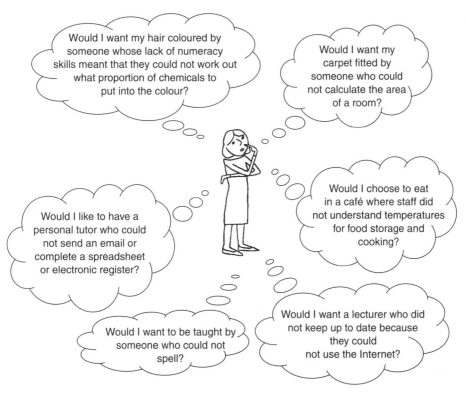

You are likely to have responded 'no' to all these questions.

The Wolf Report on Vocational Education (2011a) highlighted the fact that too few 14–19 year olds achieve English and Maths GCSE at grades A*–C and considered these fundamental to young people's employment and education prospects. The government's response to the Wolf report commits to 'Ensur[ing] that all young people study and achieve in English and Mathematics, ideally to GCSE A*–C, by the age of 19' (Department for Education, 2011b: 3, 9).

Now the ultimate aim is achievement of Level 2 in English and Mathematics whatever curriculum a young person may be following. From 2012/2013, for example, all apprentices will be taking either GCSE or Functional Skills qualifications, and all Apprenticeship providers are required to support Apprentices in progressing towards Level 2 achievement in English and Maths.

If you intend to gain a teaching qualification you should already have high levels of skills in your own subject specialism. You are not expected to be a teacher of English, Maths or ICT but it is certainly the case that you will need to support some learners to develop these skills to a level that allows them to achieve their desired qualifications.

As the Wolf Report highlighted, learners with Functional Skills which are below Level 2 can find this a barrier to achievement of their goals, particularly on Level 2 vocational programmes. It is, therefore, particularly important for you as a teacher to develop awareness of the Functional Skills below Level 2 of the Qualifications and Credit Framework.

What does the curriculum look like at lower levels?

Literacy Core Curriculum

Level	At this level someone can:
Level 1	Follow a simple written procedure, fill in an application form
Entry Level 3	Obtain information on the telephone, read job adverts, write a short letter
Entry Level 2	Fill in a simple form
Entry Level 1	Follow a one-step verbal instruction, read common signs, write name and address

Numeracy Core Curriculum

Level	At this level someone can:
Level 1	Read timetables, follow directions to mix substances in proportion, estimate distances on a map using scales
Entry Level 3	Use a map to find a location
Entry Level 2	Use simple measuring scales
Entry Level 1	Key in a telephone number

ICT Core Curriculum

Level	At this level someone can:
Level 1	Enter, organise, develop, format and bring together information to suit context and purpose in the form of (a) text and tables, (b) images, (c) numbers, (d) records
Entry Level 3	Enter and develop information to suit purpose in the form of (a) text, (b) images, (c) numbers
Entry Level 2	Enter and edit small amounts of simple information for a simple purpose
Entry Level 1	Enter and edit simple information

Do not assume your learners have a certain level of Functional Skills. Research by Paul Martinez (Martinez and Munday, 1998) showed when one college screened Level 3 students, 6 per cent were at or below Level 1 in literacy and 17 per cent in numeracy. Other organisations have come up with similar findings.

> ## Activity 12.1
>
> Why do you think that learners do not place significant value on the development of their Functional Skills provision?
>
> (You may want to refer back to Chapter 4 on motivation in order to respond.)

Many learners who are motivated to acquire vocational skills to access employment are much less motivated to focus on Functional Skills. Let us take the example of the achievement of GCSEs or Functional Skills qualifications as a mandatory part of gaining an Apprenticeship. Some apprentices have negative attitudes towards Functional Skills, either because they cannot see the relevance or because they have previously experienced failure in this area and may have managed to hide deficiencies for many years. Some learners consider practical experience to be far more important; this affects their motivation. Whilst learners may realise that they will need to communicate effectively when at work, for example to deal with customers, they are not necessarily convinced of the particular value of Functional Skills in helping them to do this. It is possible that these negative attitudes can be reinforced if not dealt with in an appropriate manner.

Mapping and embedding Functional Skills

When you identify those areas in your subject where your learners will need to use specific Functional Skills and then find these specific competences on the associated curriculum, we refer to this process as **mapping**.

Making use of naturally occurring activities in your sessions to help learners develop Functional Skills is called embedding Functional Skills; they are there, but attention is not necessarily drawn to them. You will be able to provide learners with opportunities to practise Functional Skills where this fits with the vocational area that you are teaching. When learners receive English, Maths and ICT support completely separately from their vocational studies, the Functional Skills have not been integrated and are 'non-embedded'.

Although it is important to remember that you are not a Functional Skills specialist and it is not your role to teach Functional Skills, hopefully the discussion above has started you thinking about how you could support your learners in meeting the Functional Skills demands of your subject.

Benefits of embedding Functional Skills

Research has been undertaken (Casey et al., 2006) to examine the impact of embedded approaches to language, literacy and numeracy. The sample consisted of 1,916 learners in health and social care, hair and beauty therapy, construction, business and engineering at Levels 1 and 2. Where Functional Skills had been embedded, results showed:

- 16% better staying on rates
- More positive attitude to literacy, language and numeracy
- 26% higher success rates on Level 2 courses than those on non-embedded courses
- Better achievement on literacy (up 43%) and numeracy (up 26%) qualifications than on non-embedded courses.

Embedding does have impact. Evidence suggests that vocational and Functional Skills specialists working together are likely to be most effective in helping learners to achieve. Work done by teachers who specialise in English, Maths and ICT is a big part of the solution but there is much that you can do, working in partnership, to ensure the success of your learners.

In most institutions you will find a named person responsible for Functional Skills support. If you work in a college there is likely to be a learning support service(s) with a focus on English, Maths and ICT development. This means that you are not on your own.

- You should be able to consult a Functional Skills specialist when you need advice.
- You will be able to refer learners to cross-college discrete Functional Skills programmes – English, Maths or ICT – in which learners will be taught by specialists.
- On some vocational courses, arrangements can be put in place so that additional learning support is provided in your teaching environment. A Functional Skills specialist could work alongside you and your learners.

Learners can benefit from support by specialists in literacy, language, numeracy and ICT outside your teaching specialism. It is therefore important that you know what support is available to your learners and signpost this effectively to them.

But there is also much that you can do, working in partnership with specialists, to ensure the success of your learners. Integration may be a challenge, but if learners can develop Functional Skills in a vocational context, it becomes relevant for them and worthwhile for you! There will be scope for many naturally occurring activities in your sessions to develop Functional Skills. Functional Skills experts may provide you with advice and support to identify opportunities in your session plans for your learners to develop increasingly higher levels of Functional Skills. The following case study provides an example of how this can be achieved.

🗁 Case study

On a Painting and Decorating course, the teacher worked with a Functional Skills specialist to produce an integrated assignment. The assignment was in four parts A–D; an extract from this is given below.

This enabled learners to achieve the performance criteria of their subject qualification and at the same time to meet elements of the selected Functional Skills requirements.

Assignment

Part C:
Describe an accident using an Accident Report Form

Vocational performance criteria	Functional Skills elements
Comply with all emergency procedures in accordance with organisational policy	Judge how much to write and the level of detail to include
	Present information and ideas in a logical sequence
	Use format and structure to organise writing for different purposes
	Follow and contribute to discussions on a range of straightforward topics

Part D:
Make a list of people who would be involved in investigating an accident

Vocational performance criteria	Functional Skills elements
Comply with all emergency procedures in accordance with organisational policy	Use format and structure for different purposes
	Present information and ideas in a logical sequence and provide further detail and development to clarify or confirm understanding

Successful completion of this assignment will provide evidence of the ability to:
Write two different types of documents
Read and summarise
Give a small talk

Adapted from DfES, 2005 Materials for Embedded Learning

⊞ Activity 12.2

Thinking of your subject specialism, identify instances within the teaching of your subject when learners can demonstrate competence in:

English – reading, writing, speaking, listening

Maths – number, measures, shapes and spaces, handling data

ICT – use of ICT, finding and selecting information, developing and presenting communication through a task or practical activity

Think of a new activity where you could incorporate more than one of these Functional Skills into a subject-related task.

Achieving success

To have the maximum impact in your approach to Functional Skills it is worth considering the following factors:

Checklist for success in Functional Skills

Learners

☑ Get to know your learners.
☑ Do not assume competence from any level of learner for literacy, language, numeracy or ICT.
☑ Make full use of initial assessment and induction to produce Individual Learning Plans.
☑ Use multisensory lessons, because the more senses are involved the more you can tap into learners' preferences.
☑ Think how things can be explained as simply as possible.
☑ Discuss links between Functional Skills development, vocational success and personal aspirations.

If working with specialist Functional Skills staff

☑ Develop strong working relationships with staff supporting English, Maths or ICT development, and arrive at a shared understanding of the value of Functional Skills.
☑ Ensure specialist Functional Skills staff understand the demands of the vocational course and its vocabulary.
☑ Encourage an awareness in specialist staff of learners' vocational goals.
☑ Promote aspects of teaching and learning that connect Functional Skills to vocational content.

In your organisation

☑ Find out about your organisation's approach to Functional Skills.
☑ If you are planning induction make sure your learners are fully aware of the support available.
☑ Try to timetable Functional Skills so that the subject is adjacent to vocational skills; not on a different day or at the end of a long training day.
☑ Take up training opportunities to develop your expertise in supporting the development of Functional Skills.

All this will demonstrate your commitment to Functional Skills. Working alongside specialist Functional Skills staff you will be helping learners to achieve their full potential.

Focus on your own skills

In order to support your learners most effectively it is useful to review your own Functional Skills. These skills are also a matter of concern if you wish to gain the current qualified teacher status in the lifelong learning sector (QTLS) as there is a requirement that you are able to function at least to Level 2 in terms of your own literacy, numeracy and ICT ability and can evidence your own skills at this level in English and Maths.

This level is intended to enable you to provide opportunities for your own learners to further develop their competence in speaking, listening, reading, writing, number and computer skills at the level required for their specific qualifications (see *'Addressing literacy, language, numeracy and ICT needs in education and training: defining the minimum core of teachers' knowledge, understanding and personal skills'* http://www. excellencegateway.org.uk/node/12019).

In arriving at this stage of this book you will have practised or used existing Functional Skills and will have demonstrated competence in some of the 'Minimum Core' requirements.

Activity 12.3

Can you recall any instance in this book where you have needed to use specific skills in English, Maths or ICT?

To read the *Sun* newspaper requires a reading age of seven. To read and digest this book requires a considerably more advanced vocabulary and consequently a higher reading age. There is a significant relationship between the language learners can use and their development of new thinking. As you have acquired educational vocabulary it will have enabled you to analyse and reflect on your teaching in a way that you may not have been able to previously.

Literacy skills were also required to understand the vocabulary in Chapter 5. For example, the word 'mnemonic' is used; the spelling, if not the word itself, may have been new to some readers. You will then see the meaning given afterwards in more accessible language, 'memory aid'. Chapter 10 may have stretched some readers' literacy boundaries. In this case the explanation of the concept of 'validity' comes first, before what may be a new word for some readers is introduced. In these examples we have built in material that may promote new learning for you.

To meet the requirements of Level 2 in Literacy you need to:

Understand that specialist fields of knowledge, skills and interest have an associated technical vocabulary. (RW.L2)

As you have worked through this book you will have encountered the specialist vocabulary associated with teaching, for example:

- The taxonomy of learning objectives in Chapter 6
- Vocabulary used in a way specific to education in the chapters related to assessment and evaluation.

You may have thought, 'too much jargon!', but being able to use specialist language enables us to communicate with each other as part of a wider professional community. Think about your own specialism: you will need to be able to identify and perhaps be more alert to similar reactions from your learners.

At several points in this book you have needed to understand how a graph is laid out and what the data on each axis tell you, in order to absorb the information.

Know how to interpret information from bar charts, pie charts and line graphs with more than one line. (HD1.L2) Level 2 Criteria for Numeracy

In a teaching situation you should be able to spot those learners who have difficulty interpreting such information and be able to introduce other activities, related to your subject, that use this type of presentation.

An example of developing use of ICT skills can be found at the end of each chapter, where it is proposed that you access web-based material. This is in line with:

Use appropriate search techniques and design queries to locate relevant information. (F1/L2:4.2) Level 2 Criteria for ICT

We hope you will now appreciate, from the examples above, that we have mapped the English, Maths and ICT requirements that you will face and then aimed to help you move towards achieving them through the material and activities in the book. We have intentionally embedded some Level 2 Functional Skills; the best embedding occurs when it is fully integrated and relevant to the learning goal, and hopefully that has been your experience.

We would not claim to be Functional Skills experts, and, for those of you without a Level 2 in English and Maths, we have certainly not been able to embed sufficient development of skills in this book for you to meet the requirements of a GCSE. However, we have deliberately aimed to support such development.

Having considered initial assessment in Chapter 6 you will appreciate that you will need to review your own skills in English and Maths and consider whether, and how, you need to develop these.

Chapter summary

The main points covered in this chapter are:

✓ Functional Skills are the core elements of English, Mathematics and ICT that enable individuals to function effectively and independently in life, education and work.
✓ The government requires all 16–18 year olds to have achieved or be working towards Level 2 competence in English and Maths, evidenced through GCSEs Grades A*–C or Functional Skills qualifications.
✓ A learner with good Functional Skills is more likely to be successful on their chosen vocational or academic programme.
✓ Mapping involves analysing the specific Functional Skills needed to succeed on a learning programme.
✓ Embedding requires you to make use of naturally occurring activities in your subject specialism to help learners develop Functional Skills.
✓ Working in partnership with Functional Skills specialists enables you to integrate Functional Skills development in your teaching situation.
✓ Awareness of learning support available in your institution allows you to be effective in signposting learners to this.
✓ You can use the checklist of Success Factors above.
✓ An analysis of your own Functional Skills will enable you to plan any development you require.

→ References

Casey, H. et al. (2006) *'You Wouldn't Expect a Maths Teacher to Teach Plastering …': Embedding Literacy, Language and Numeracy on Post-16 Vocational Programmes – the Impact on Learning and Achievement*. London: NRDC.

Department for Business, Innovation and Skills (2011) *Skills for Life Survey: Headline Findings*. BIS Research Paper no. 57.

Department for Education (2011a) *Review of Vocational Education – The Wolf Report*. Available at: https://www.education.gov.uk/publications/eOrderingDownload/Wolf-Review.pdf

Department for Education (2011b) *Wolf Review of Vocational Education: Government Response*. Available at: https://www.education.gov.uk/publications/eOrderingDownload/Wolf-Review_Response.pdf

Martinez, P. and Munday, F. (1998) *9000 Voices: Student Persistence and Drop-out in Further Education*. London: FEDA.

📖 Further reading

Wallace, S. (eds) (2010) *The Lifelong Learning Sector Reflective Reader*. Exeter: Learning Matters.

Chapter 5 by Sheine Peart provides the underlying context to the issue of literacy and numeracy, outlining the teacher's responsibilities in these areas.

Keeley-Brown, L. and Price, A. (2011) *Numeracy for QTLS*. London: Pearson.
Part 1 provides a useful focus on the barriers experienced by learners when approaching number.

Learning Matters have a series of three books covering Literacy, Numeracy and ICT. You can locate these from the link below.
http://www.uk.sagepub.com/productSearch.nav?subject=C00&subject=CK0&publisher=%22Learning+Matters%22&sortBy=defaultPubDate+desc&pager.offset=20

Useful websites

You can find the latest standards for Functional Skills at this link:
http://www.ofqual.gov.uk/downloads/category/68-functional-skills-subject-criteria

You can find the latest government announcements on Functional Skills and government policy at these links:
http://www.education.gov.uk/schools/teachingandlearning/qualifications/functionalskills/a0064058/functional-skills

Department of Business, Innovation and Skills (2011) *New Challenges, New Changes; Further Education and Skills System Reform: Building a World Class Skills System*. London: BIS.

13

Developing session plans

Chapter overview

When you have worked through this chapter on developing session plans you will be able to:

- Recognise the three functions of a session plan
- Identify what should be included in a plan
- Manage time effectively
- Describe the different phases of a teaching session and what is included in each
- Self-evaluate a teaching session in a systematic manner
- Identify session formats appropriate to either a group or workshop setting

The purpose of planning

We have already agreed that normally, whatever we do, we do it better if we plan it first. Planning is part of our everyday life. If we go on a trip, we first get out the appropriate map and plan our route. If we go shopping, we first write a list of the things we need to buy. If we want to build a house, we first draw up the appropriate plans. Similarly, any form of teaching, whether it be a theoretical, practical or attitudinally based subject, works better if we first draw up a plan of our intentions.

The word *intentions* is important here because a plan is drawn up before the event. It maps out what we anticipate will happen. If we put some thought into this and consider all the different factors that will affect the plan, then our intentions and what happens on the day should be fairly close. Often, however, events take a turn which we could not have anticipated.

 Activity 13.1

Note any unexpected events or conditions that might cause you to deviate from your session plan.

Typically, some of the following may occur:

- The learners know more or less than we thought
- The learners are held up and arrive late for the session
- The resources we require are unavailable
- Someone comes up with a good idea that is worth pursuing.

Do we ignore these or do we take these into account? Let us consider our other examples of planning. If we started off on our journey and found there was heavy traffic, would we sit in it because our original plan said that was our route? We could do, but it would make more sense to adapt our route to meet these unexpected circumstances. Similarly, if we were building a house we may alter our plans to take advantage of new building materials, rather than stick to the old materials just because they were on our original plan.

Plans we write for teaching, then, are not scripts that must be followed to the letter. Plans are guidelines that can be used flexibly to ensure a more effective session. We will explore the idea of flexibility further as we progress through this chapter. First we need to identify our purpose in writing these plans.

Session plans have three functions that refer to different stages of the teaching process:

Before

By writing a session plan, we are prepared and confident before we teach. Even if it is a new area of teaching for us, when we come to deliver it for the first time we have already delivered it 'in our head'. The session plan contains a list of all of the resources we need. By reference to it we can be confident we have everything ready.

During

The session plan is a checklist, not only of resources, but also of what you are to deliver and how. It provides a memory aid of all aspects of the delivery of the session which you can refer to at any stage. It helps us to stick to the 'best' sequence, reminds us of the main points we wish to make and helps us to manage time. Generally, it ensures that, as far as circumstances allow, we deliver the session as we had intended.

After

If you repeat a teaching session, will you start from scratch in your planning? Not if you have a record of a previous occasion to refer back to. This is the third function of the session plan; it provides you with a record of what you have done. When you plan this session again you can look back to this previous session plan and use it or change it to fit the demands of the new context. You may make changes based on your experience of the previous occasion. This is a notion we will pursue further when we look at evaluation.

There are two factors that are important with regard to this 'after' function:

1 You will need more detail on a lesson plan than is necessary just to deliver it in the 'during' phase if the plan is to be an effective record. Key words may trigger thoughts whilst the plan and its contents are still fairly fresh in your mind, but if you come to teach the same or a similar session at a later stage, maybe six months later, this will undoubtedly not be the case. The plan needs sufficient detail to be able to act as a 'standalone' record that does not rely on memories of the session.

2 It is important, early on in your teaching career, to develop a system for storing your session plans. If you do this electronically it will allow you to 'cut and paste' between different plans, and add to or alter existing plans; recycling is common and when applied to teaching plans, allows us to derive the greatest return from the efforts we have made in writing them in the first place.

Planning decisions

The plan is a record of the decisions we have arrived at in planning that particular session.

Your decisions will cause you to ask the following sorts of questions when you are planning:

- Where will the session take place?
- How many learners will there be?
- What do they already know, what can they already do?
- What are the aims and objectives of the session?
- Are they relevant and realistic to the learners?
- What information will I have to impart?
- How much time can I spend on each topic?
- What methods will I be using?
- What resources are available?
- How can I check that learning has occurred?
- How will I know if the session has been successful?

You will not be able to remember the answers to all these questions when you are delivering the session and your attention is occupied by more immediate concerns; this information is therefore best recorded. The act of recording it also helps you to structure your thoughts and decisions. This allows you to be more systematic in your approach to planning.

Activity 13.2

Note anything else you would want to record relating to your subject specialism.

Having decided what to record, the next consideration is the format or layout of the plan. An example of a lesson plan follows.

Format 1 – Group plan

Course:	Group:	
Venue:	Time:	Date:
Topic/Title:	Aims:	

Learning outcomes:	How each outcome will be assessed:	Checklist of resources required:

Notes on learners:	Differentiation strategies:	Links to Functional Skills:
Self-evaluation:		

Achieving Your PTLLS Award, 2nd edition © Mary Francis and Jim Gould 2013

Time	Development	Delivery		Resources	Assessment
		Teacher activity	Learner activity		
	Introduction				
	Middle				
	End				

Structuring a session plan

Possibly you have a lesson plan format that your employing institution either advises or requires you to use, or perhaps your course has a recommended format, but ideally you are in a position whereby you can devise a plan to fit your own particular circumstances and preferences. Individual session plans are taken from a scheme of work, which in turn is a breakdown of the syllabus to which you will be working. At this stage we are only concerned with planning at session level, and so you will find it helpful to look at the example session plans on pages 170–171 and 179. The first of these is the type of format that would be used when teaching a group, probably in a classroom setting. Quite often, however, although we have a group of learners, they could be working independently on individual projects, possibly in a workshop setting; the second format later in the chapter suggests how planning might be recorded in this type of situation.

You will notice that the sample plans using Format 1 record two types of information. The first page relates to the context of the session and the second to its delivery.

The context of the session

- Where and when the session will be conducted
- What is to be learned (objectives) and how it is to be assessed
- The main resources required
- Who the learners will be and any particular characteristics of individual learners or the group as a whole that need to be considered
- Differentiation strategies to be employed
- Any Functional Skills needs
- The resources required
- What has been learned as a result of teaching this session.

The context is concerned mainly with the **Before** and **After** functions of the session plan.

Before encourages you to think about the objectives of the teaching session, the learners who are to achieve these and how you propose to check that learning is indeed taking place as the session proceeds. You will want to write SMART objectives that are achievable and relevant to your learners and ensure that the session is inclusive in its planning. The plan also demonstrates how you have considered the Functional Skills needs of both your subject and your learners. The checklist of resources helps ensure you have everything you need.

What you record in the section on self-evaluation informs the planning of future sessions and so also fulfils an **After** function.

The **During** functions are mainly to do with the delivery on the day and we shall look at these issues next.

The delivery of the session

You will find the following items related to the delivery of the teaching session on the example plans:

- Timing
- The development of content and the sequence in which it will be delivered
- The activities employed at each stage of the session
- When and how learning resources will be used
- Checks on learning.

Decisions concerning these items are best recorded in columns on a session plan as this makes it easier for you to focus on the specific items you require. We will look at some of these in more depth.

Timing

Time is the most precious commodity in a teaching session. There is rarely sufficient time to cover all that learners need, in the depth you wish. So, as with any other precious commodity, what time is available should be put to best use. We manage this by allocating blocks of time to each area to be covered.

Often our estimates of time will not be as accurate as we would like, particularly if we are dealing with a new topic. Consider the following sequence:

What happens if the introduction overruns and we do not start Activity 1 until 9.50? Activity 2 then takes until 10.45 and our times are already inaccurate. This is not disastrous by any means. Sticking to the times is not our key concern; our main priority is that learners achieve the objectives. There are only two times that have to be strictly observed: the **Start** time and the **Finish** time. If this is so, why write the other times on the plan?

Suppose you have to travel 100km in two hours. You start off at the allotted time and you reach the halfway point in only 45 minutes. If you complete the journey at the same speed, you know you will arrive 30 minutes early. You have the option then, of travelling more slowly or altering your plans and taking a more 'scenic route'. Alternatively, if it takes you 75 minutes to reach the halfway

9.30	Introduction
9.40	Activity 1
10.05	Activity 2
10.30	Break
10.45	Activity 3
11.20	Draw conclusions
11.30	End

point, you know that you will have to go faster or find a shorter route to arrive at your destination on time. In both cases it is important that you are aware of the situation while there is still an opportunity to respond. If you do not find out until the end of the journey, you are not in a position to do anything about it.

A similar argument applies to the times on session plans. These can be compared to 'distance markers' rather than deadlines to be adhered to. By being aware of whether we are behind time, on time or ahead of time at any stage during the session, we can adjust our pace and delivery so we can stick to those two important times of **Start** and **Finish**. The purpose of recording times on a plan is to enable more effective and flexible management of time, not to provide a timetable that must be rigidly followed.

One way of achieving this is by classifying the content of the session in terms of relative importance, and we often use the categories of that which learners 'must know', 'should know' and 'could know' to accomplish this.

- **'Must know'** refers to material that is essential to the achievement of the learning objectives, and preserving this is a priority in all adjustments we make.
- **'Should know'** is useful because it elaborates or extends the 'must know' category. Every effort should be made to cover this material but if our timing goes seriously awry, we will consider leaving it out to preserve the 'must know'.
- **'Could know'** refers to material that might be helpful to the learners because it illustrates or extends the previous categories, but is not essential to achievement of the learning objectives. We will include it if time permits but be prepared to leave it out in favour of the other, more important categories.

Timing the delivery of sessions improves with practice; classifying the material we intend to include in the session allows us to be flexible with our timing, ensuring essential points are covered and we respond to the needs of learners more effectively.

Content and order

It is useful to think of sessions having a **Beginning – Middle – End** pattern. We will consider each part of this structure in turn.

The **Beginning** of the session is where we make our initial impact and set the scene for what is to follow. Exactly what is included at this stage will depend upon factors such as:

- Is this a 'one-off' session or part of a sequence?
- Do you know the learners and do they know you?
- Are learners familiar with the environment?

There are, however, a number of features that we might expect to see in a Beginning.

 **Activity 13.3**

What do you consider needs to take place at the beginning of a session?

In general, the following might be included in a Beginning of a 'one-off' session or a first meeting between you and the group:

Introductions

☑ Introduce yourself – give a little relevant background to establish credibility.
☑ Give the learners an opportunity to introduce each other.

Practical matters

☑ Give the location of any appropriate facilities.
☑ Explain any Health and Safety requirements and show Fire Exits.
☑ Complete any necessary paperwork.

Setting the scene

☑ Introduce the topic – what will be covered (or possibly not covered).
☑ Show how it links to what learners already know.
☑ Introduce any ground rules – acceptable procedures for this session.

Arousing interest

☑ Explain the relevance and benefits of the teaching you will be delivering.
☑ Present an enthusiastic role model.

If you and the group already know each other and the session is part of a sequence, a more likely procedure would be:

1 Involve learners straight away with an active start to the session – a short, sharp exercise can be given to learners as they enter the room which is sufficiently flexible in its layout to allow you to stop it at a convenient moment; perhaps a 'gap-fill' exercise or quiz which involves a recap of the previous session. This

allows you to integrate latecomers into the session with minimum disruption and affords an opportunity for some initial individual contact.

2   Bring the exercise to a halt and acknowledge the work that has been completed before formally recapping previous learning, perhaps using question and answer. Next outline the proposed outcomes of the session, their relevance and usefulness and the types of activities that are to be used.

The *Middle* of the session covers the delivery of the main content and introduces any activities or exercises that are planned. The content should be delivered in a logical sequence and preferably be split into smaller sub-sections.

In general, new information should build on existing knowledge and experience. Learners take in information most easily if a basic, simple idea is introduced to start off with that can then be built up to a higher level of complexity.

As seen in Chapter 8, attention spans tend to be longer when more 'active' teaching methods are employed. Conversely, teaching methods where learners take a more 'passive' role are less effective in attracting and maintaining attention. Although the level of attention will normally fall to some degree as the session progresses, a variety of methods is important in maintaining attention and concentration levels at their highest levels. This could be achieved through a sequence such as:

1   Initial explanation and introduction of new material with some question and answer
2   Some form of exercise/group work/pair work/ using the new material
3   Learning check, summary and link to the next stage of the session
4   Repeat a similar pattern until the session objectives are achieved.

This pattern can be adapted to suit your own style but, when supported by appropriate resources, should suit most circumstances.

Endings, like Beginnings, often include a number of common features.

Activity 13.4

What would you include at the end of a session?

The *End* of the session is where all of the threads are drawn together and the important points highlighted. In ending a session, you might:

- Review the session as a whole
- Ask questions on the main points covered
- Take any questions on matters arising out of the session
- Suggest follow-up exercises
- Show how this session links with future sessions.

Considering the sequence and content of a session enables us to develop a sound structure for the delivery of our teaching.

Self-evaluation

Sometimes a session goes well and sometimes, despite our best efforts, it does not. Whichever the case might be, we can learn from every session we deliver and use that learning to improve future sessions. We achieve this through a process of evaluation. Evaluation can be defined as:

> *The collecting of information about the sessions we deliver that allows us to make informed decisions concerning our teaching, leading to the improvement of future sessions.*

Information necessary for evaluation can be obtained from a number of sources:

- Yourself
- Your learners
- Colleagues.

And by a number of means:

- Self-rating checklists – used by you after completing a session
- Oral feedback – individual and group discussion with learners or colleagues
- Written feedback – evaluation sheets completed by learners
- Checklists completed by colleagues.

Most often, however, the kind of evaluation we engage in is self-evaluation when, after the session, we ask ourselves a number of questions and record our answers on the lesson plan. This acts as a reminder of how this session went and what we have learned from the experience that can inform our planning if we deliver this, or a similar session again. The kind of questions we would ask ourselves are:

1 What were the significant features of this session? Which parts of it were well received? In which parts did you have evidence that students were learning? Which parts of the session proved difficult or generally did not go as well?
2 Why? What were the reasons behind the more and less successful aspects of the session?
3 If these are the reasons, what might I do differently next time I teach either this session or this group?

Sometimes, prior to the session, we might have an idea of specific aspects that it would be useful to evaluate, giving our self-evaluation a more structured approach.

Activity 13.5

What areas would you find it useful to consider in your self-evaluation?

Self-evaluation contributes to the *After* function of the session plan when it acts as a record of what has been done. When we come to deliver this or a similar session again we know not only what we planned to do, but also how effective this was, and we are in a better position to think through any changes that might be appropriate next time.

We have now considered in some detail what to think about when constructing a session plan and how to record these decisions. To help you in writing your own plans, you might find it useful to refer to the checklist below.

Session plan checklist

Does your plan contain the following?

- ☑ Clearly stated learning objectives.
- ☑ An indication of differentiation strategies to be used.
- ☑ Identification of Functional Skills related to this topic.
- ☑ Clear introduction.
- ☑ Logical progression.
- ☑ Timing.
- ☑ Variety of appropriate teaching methods and learning activities.
- ☑ Plenty of learner participation.
- ☑ Variety of appropriate resources.
- ☑ Checks on learning.
- ☑ Something to leave out or add in.

Planning format for individual learning through a project or workshop

In a project or workshop situation, although you may start and end the session by addressing the group as a whole, learners will be working individually for the vast majority of the time. The exact nature of their learning will depend upon the task or activity in which they are engaged. Outcomes, activities, assessment and resources will vary from learner to learner, and so planning has to take account of this. The following Format 2 provides a way of planning which is personalised and takes account of the needs of each individual learner. The top line gives some

Format 2 – Workshop plan

	Course:	Module:	Venue:
	Date:	Date:	Date:
Learner 1	Outcome/Target:	Outcome/Target:	Outcome/Target:
	Resource requirements:	Resource requirements:	Resource requirement:
	Progress/Evaluation:	Progress/Evaluation:	Progress/Evaluation:
Learner 2	Outcome/Target:	Outcome/Target:	Outcome/Target:
	Resource requirements:	Resource requirements:	Resource requirements:
	Progress/Evaluation:	Progress/Evaluation:	Progress/Evaluation:

 Achieving Your PTLLS Award, 2nd edition © Mary Francis and Jim Gould 2013

context, but the plan is mainly concerned with identifying individual targets and tracking progress.

In the case of Learner 1, the plan would be filled in as follows:

- The *date* is the date of the particular session.
- The *Outcome/Target* box is used to record whatever it is that the individual learner is to achieve in the session. It can be phrased as a learning outcome, a task, a series of short tasks or a short-term goal, depending upon which of these is more appropriate to the kind of session being run. Whatever the choice, it should provide Learner 1 with a sense of purpose and a structure to work from, and can be reviewed as the session progresses.
- Towards the end of the session, time needs to be made to meet briefly with each learner and review progress. At this stage an entry is made in the *Progress/ Evaluation* box, summarising what has been learned, progress with the task, obstacles encountered and overcome, or whatever is deemed appropriate. The purpose here is to evaluate performance and identify what has been learned. This entry can be made by learners or jointly, depending upon their level of maturity and independence.
- The outcome/target for the next session can also be agreed and recorded at this stage, so learners know what they will be doing in advance and you will be aware of any resource implications which can be recorded in the resources for the next session box.

The plan for the following weeks might look like the case study below.

Case study

Learner 1 comes into the plumbing workshop. An outcome has been agreed in the previous session, so Learner 1 knows what is to be done in this session. Learner 1's first task is to identify the tools required for the job. When the tool list is prepared, it is checked with the teacher or technician, and tools are issued to Learner 1. Learner 1 then checks what he proposes to do with the teacher and then gets the 'go ahead' to start work. The teacher monitors progress	**Outcome/target:** **Install Radiators Bay 4** Hang radiators on wall. Connect flow and return pipework. Test and balance radiators
	Resource requirements: Prepare tool list. List materials including type and size of radiator valves
Shortly before the end of the session, the teacher discusses progress with Learner 1 and they agree the outcome/target for the next session and record this on the next section of the plan	**Progress/Evaluation:** Radiators hung correctly although getting them level took longer than expected. Continue with pipework and testing next session

Following weeks look like this:

Outcome/Target: Continue piping and testing of radiators	Outcome/Target: Check standards for clip spacing. Fill radiators ready for testing and marking
Resource requirements: List of copper tube and fittings required	Resource requirements Current standards for testing information. Clips to be ordered for stores – state how many you will need
Progress/Evaluation: Radiators piped up with correct valves and size of pipe. A few more clips are required to comply with current standards. As soon as this is done we are ready for testing	Progress/Evaluation: Installation completed correctly. Very neat job. One small water leak, which was repaired promptly. Pipe work connected to boiler. Radiators balanced and working correctly. Job photographed and stripped out. Ready to progress to water cylinder activity next session

As learners become familiar with the process, they can become more involved in the planning of their own learning, and possibly reach a stage when the process can be handed over to them.

In the workplace Learner 1 will have to plan what is to be achieved in the morning or by the end of the day in order to work effectively and cost jobs accurately. By encouraging learners to negotiate and reflect on what they want to achieve we contribute towards the development of this skill as well as giving learners some control over their learning.

You should now be able to produce a well-structured session plan to use in your teaching, whether for a whole group or for individuals. The suggested formats can be changed and adapted to meet your own specific needs and further developed as you become more familiar with the processes and demands of planning. Further examples, which have been completed, are provided in Appendix 2.

Planning does improve with practice!

Chapter summary

The main points covered in this chapter are:

- ✓ Plans record our *intentions* for a particular session.
- ✓ Session plans have three functions – Before, During and After – and the requirements of each influence how we complete the plan.
- ✓ Session plans record both the context within which a session occurs and the intended strategy to be adopted.
- ✓ Timings on a session plan act as reference points rather than as a timetable.
- ✓ A well-structured session contains a defined Beginning, Middle and End, each of which has a specific purpose.
- ✓ Self-evaluation is the process of reviewing all aspects of the planned session with a view to improvement.
- ✓ Different planning formats are used for whole group and workshop settings.

📖 Further reading

A number of general texts cover planning. Two of these are:

Le Versha, L. and Nicholls, G. (2003) *Teaching at Post 16*. London: Kogan Page.

Chapter 8 gives a planning format and discusses a number of planning issues, particularly differentiation.

Reece, I. and Walker, S. (2007) *Teaching Training and Learning: A Practical Guide* (6th edn). Sunderland: Business Education Publishers.

Useful background on planning and some other formats for consideration are to be found in the section on 'Planning Learning' in Chapter 1.

Scales, P. (2008) *Teaching in the Lifelong Learning Sector*. Maidenhead: Open University Press.

Chapter 4 'Planning for Teaching and Learning' contains example scheme of work and lesson plan formats.

Sotto, E. (2007) *When Teaching Becomes Learning* (2nd edn). London: Continuum.

Chapter 17 looks at session planning and ties this in with assessment and evaluation.

14

Evaluating learning

Chapter overview

When you have worked through this chapter on evaluating learning you will be able to:

- Define evaluation
- Identify the purposes of evaluation
- List different methods to evaluate sessions and recognise the strengths and limitations of each
- Recognise the characteristics of a well-written questionnaire
- Draw up a personal action plan to improve your future sessions

Why evaluate?

When we assess, we are looking to see whether or not objectives have been achieved. Evaluation, whilst taking account of the results of assessment, also takes a wider view of the delivery of learning. The word evaluation relates to *value* and is concerned with questions about the worth and value of a session or programme and how it has been conducted.

When we evaluate we are looking for the answers to questions such as:

- Were the objectives appropriate and achievable?
- Were the methods selected suitable, matching both objectives and learner characteristics?
- Was the pacing of the session right?
- Were the resources used the most appropriate, and, if so, were they used to best advantage?
- Was learning checked using appropriate formal or informal methods?

The example below concerns people learning Mandarin in order to conduct business meetings in China; we can easily see from this how the assessment and evaluation processes complement each other.

Assessment at the end of the course will tell us whether or not learners can ask simple questions and give simple explanations which will be understood in China.

Evaluation might further inform us that the learners wanted more time to talk, that they would have liked sessions to be livelier, with more work in pairs, and that they felt they could have benefited from extra study between sessions.

The key purpose of evaluation (previously defined on p. 177) is to enable us to *gather information* that gives a measure of the *effectiveness* of the delivery of learning. We can then *use* this information to *improve* future sessions or programmes that we conduct. So, evaluation often leads to:

- Changes in the design of the teaching or training we offer
- Changes in the way we deliver learning.

Evaluation therefore involves looking back over a session or programme. We gather as much evidence as we can in order to weigh up how it has gone – what its strengths and weaknesses were – with the intention of making it better next time.

The questions we have posed above are very general in nature. In order to bring about meaningful improvement we would need to consider more specific areas related to our own teaching and learning context.

Activity 14.1

What specific areas would be of particular interest to you when evaluating your own teaching?

How does your list compare with the areas for evaluation that we have identified below?

- Did learners achieve the objectives?
- Content of your programme – was it relevant to the learners' work situation?
- Programme objectives – were they appropriate and SMART?
- Planning – did it take account of previous experience and level of understanding?
- Suitability of the facilities
- Use of visual aids and other resources
- Issues of equality
- Appropriate communication patterns
- Level of rapport with learners
- Suitability of methods of delivery
- Sequencing of materials
- Pacing of delivery
- Balance of learner and teacher activity
- Did learners make the best use of e-learning?
- Degree of learner participation

- Group management
- Responsiveness to learner need
- Attention level of learners
- Sufficient opportunities to practice
- Appropriate methods of checking learning
- Quality of feedback given to learners
- Did learners feel safe?

How to evaluate

What methods of evaluation can we use?

In order to help us identify which methods of evaluation we could use, think back to sessions or courses in which you have been involved as a learner.

Activity 14.2

How would you judge whether one of your sessions or courses had been successful?

Where would you find evidence to support your decision?

The following are some possible sources of information:

- Talking to learners
- Written feedback – participant questionnaire
- Online questionnaire
- How many learners drop out of the programme
- Feedback from an observer
- Attendance and punctuality
- Assessment results.

All of these give an indication of how the programme is progressing or has progressed. We will, of course, be forming an impression (known as formative evaluation), as we go along, by informal means such as:

- The expressions on learners' faces
- Eye contact or lack of it
- How people sit – forward or back
- Levels of learner participation
- The level of enthusiasm within the group.

These only give us impressions, however, and we normally rely on formal methods to obtain more reliable information. These formal methods tend to be used at the end of a session or programme in a summative manner.

We have already touched upon **self-evaluation** in Chapter 13, where we reflect upon our own performance. This is a necessary activity for anyone who wishes to improve their effectiveness as a teacher. Self-evaluation can, however, be rather narrow in scope, as it focuses on areas viewed only from the teacher's personal perspective. A more revealing process is to ask the learners for feedback, and this can form the basis for formal evaluation of sessions and programmes. We will examine this in more detail before briefly returning to self-evaluation at the end of this section.

To obtain the information we require, we can either ask learners directly for their opinions – spoken techniques – or have them fill in some form of evaluation questionnaire, maybe electronically – written techniques. Each approach has its own particular advantages and drawbacks. We shall consider each in turn.

Spoken techniques

It is possible for us to talk to learners individually, but this is generally a time-consuming process. We are, therefore, more likely to use some form of group technique. This has the further advantage of interaction, which may encourage learners to feed off and build upon each other's comments. There are, however, potential problems with spoken techniques.

Activity 14.3

What problems have you come across in participating in or using spoken techniques for evaluation purposes?

You may have identified some of the following problems as ones you may encounter in using spoken evaluation techniques:

Content

- Discussion centres on limited areas.

Contributions

- Everyone talks at once
- Individuals take over the evaluation
- Some learners make no contribution at all
- We may assume that individuals are talking on behalf of the group as a whole.

These problems can be largely offset by the way in which we conduct the evaluation.

Content

Often discussion can become narrow in focus or alternatively can jump from one topic to another. It helps to have some form of structure within which to collect feedback. We can broaden the discussion and help it keep focus by identifying the range of areas to be covered in advance.

To achieve this we can pose specific questions or nominate particular topics to be covered. Alternatively, we can ask our learners to come up with some headings that will provide a structure. Often, a good compromise is to use a combination of our own and learners' suggestions. Some learner participation in proposing discussion areas is desirable, to overcome the bias that we, as teachers, might otherwise impart to proceedings.

Contributions

We can employ a variety of discussion techniques to try to counter the problems identified above. You were introduced to some of these in Chapter 8 but they are used slightly differently for evaluation purposes. These will include the following:

Snowballing

In this evaluation activity we first ask learners to jot down their thoughts on the course individually on a piece of paper. They then discuss these with one other member of the group. Pairs then combine and discuss in fours. This 'doubling up' can be repeated as many times as we think appropriate. The final groups each elect a spokesperson to feed back the conclusions of their discussion. This method ensures that everyone contributes to the final evaluation and the appointment of a spokesperson de-personalises the process of giving feedback.

A round

We ask each learner in turn for a contribution. To make this exercise less threatening we can allow learners to 'pass' when their turn comes, although to some extent this defeats the purpose of having everyone make a contribution to the evaluation.

Buzz groups

We split the larger group into a series of smaller groups. The course experience is discussed in these groups and their conclusions are reported back by the nominated spokesperson at the end of the evaluation.

It is very important that we keep some record of the discussion. Ideally this should be a 'public' record that could be copied and distributed.

Written techniques

Spoken techniques can be very time-consuming and often we make use of written techniques because they are quicker and easier to administer. Written techniques can lead to more honest feedback, as learners may well feel able to commit to paper what they feel unable to tell us face-to-face. This is particularly the case if learners can respond anonymously. The most frequently used written technique is the questionnaire. There are a number of ways in which we can design a questionnaire. This will depend on whether our main aim is to collect detailed information or to collect information that we can easily collate and analyse.

In the following example you will find different questions we could ask if we wanted you, our readers, to evaluate the section so far.

---

1. Have you found this section on evaluation useful?

    YES/NO

    CLOSED

2. How useful have you found this section on evaluation? Please tick the appropriate description.

    very useful   moderately useful   not useful
    ☐   ☐   ☐

3. How useful have you found this section on evaluation to be?

    ....

4. How have you found this section on evaluation?

    ....

    OPEN

Types of questions used in questionnaires

From these examples you can see that questions can be closed in nature, requiring only a straightforward 'yes' or 'no', or open-ended, encouraging a detailed response. The first question is the most closed and the last the most open. Closed questions provide us with limited information, but have the advantage that we can collate the responses easily. We would be more likely to use this type of question if we had a large number of questionnaires. The last question is the most open and therefore provides a rich, detailed source of data. This does mean, however, that it can be difficult to reach overall conclusions from all the responses put together.

Often we use a combination of question types, firstly to elicit a simple response and secondly to seek further clarification if required:

---

1   Has this section on evaluation been relevant to your own teaching situation? YES/NO
2   If not, please say why and suggest how it could have been improved.

Whatever type of question we use, the devising and writing of evaluation questionnaires requires careful thought. The following points provide some guidance.

When writing questionnaires remember to:

☑ Keep questions simple and concise.
☑ Leave sufficient space for answers.
☑ Make the layout consistent.
☑ Make the design attractive.
☑ Limit the number of questions.
☑ Ask easier questions first.
☑ Cover everything you want to find out about.
☑ Thank the learner for their contribution.

As teachers, we can select evaluation methods that are appropriate for our learners, session or programme. We can choose between formal and informal methods of evaluation. It is helpful if you can use a range of techniques to collect information about your programmes and evaluate your learners' progress.

Activity 14.4

Which evaluation techniques would be suitable for your learners and your programme?

Returning to self-evaluation, it may now be useful to consider in more detail exactly what we might be taking into account in this process. Some teachers make their own checklist to use after each session. You will undoubtedly find it helpful to devise a checklist of your own which fits your own particular context. You may find it useful to consult the examples that follow on pages 190 and 191.

Session evaluation form

During this session, what seemed to go well was:

I think this was because:

What didn't appear to go well was:

I think this was because:

If I repeat this session

I will do again:

I will change:

Checklist for evaluating a session

How effective was.......	Very effective	Effective	Satisfactory	Ineffective
Introduction to the session				
Making outcomes clear to learner				
Structure of the session				
Emphasis placed on key points				
Pacing				
Use of voice				
Level of interest maintained				
Use of questioning				
Balance of teacher/ learner activity				
Motivating learners				
Level of participation				
Learners' use of safe working practices				
Types of teaching materials				
Use of teaching materials				
Use of e-resources				
Checking on learning				
Summarising and bringing session to an end				

Action planning

So far we have looked at the first part of evaluation – gathering information. Next we will consider how we might put this information to use in improving our teaching.

There is no point in evaluating a session or programme unless we follow up the results of the evaluation and plan for improvement. If things have gone well we will want to build on these; if things have not gone well we will want to consider changes to implement on future occasions.

This is where an action plan can be helpful. Its purpose is to:

- Ensure that we learn from the experience that we have had
- Establish priorities
- Identify responsibilities
- Establish the timescale within which changes should occur.

In our action plan we would therefore specify what should be done, by whom and by when. An example is provided here which you can adapt to suit your professional situation.

Action Planning

Issue	Change	By when?
Learners lost concentration after 45 minutes	Review activities and plan to increase active learning methods	Next session
Learners unable to perform skill	Redo skills analysis and plan a spot demonstration of difficult section	Next skill session
Ran out of materials for practice session	Technician to order materials required 2 weeks ahead	Next month
Learners found it difficult to cope with simulated practice conducted in the training room	Re-plan so that practice and assessment takes place in the workplace	Before next course

Action plans can also provide a useful method of bringing sessions or programmes to a conclusion. In this context, we are talking about learners drawing up their own individual action plans. They are encouraged to summarise what they have learned and how they will put this to use in their own working environment.

This can be done informally or can be made more formal by learners filling in an individual action plan that they then take away with them. It may differ from the action planning example given above, as its function is rather different. A suggested layout for an individual action plan is given on the next page.

Individual action plan

Name: ....   Date: ....   Session: ....

The four major points I have learned from this session are:

1.

2.

3.

4.

How I will use each of these to improve my practice:

Learning Point	How I will use it	Target Date	Completed
1			
2			
3			
4			

I will review my progress on this action plan on ....(date)

If we refer back to the purpose of evaluation we can see that action planning completes the process of evaluation, as it takes us to the stage where 'We can then *use* this information *to improve* future sessions or programmes that we conduct'. Evaluation is as crucial to the planning process as is preparation and planning. If you refer back to the Planning Cycle in Chapter 5, you will see that evaluation brings us to the end of the cycle, and informs our planning at the beginning of the next cycle.

So, it is important to evaluate the learning that takes place in our sessions and to draw up an action plan for how we might do things differently. At course or programme level a similar review is undertaken, drawing on the outcomes of evaluation, such as yours, together with statistics on the retention and achievement of learners.

Furthermore, it is critical that evaluation also takes place at an institutional level where, amongst other indicators, it will draw on the observations of staff teaching. Evaluation allows an institution, whether a college, a work-based learning provider or an adult education service, to take stock, produce a self-assessment report (SAR) and develop a quality improvement plan (QIP). These can then inform the direction of the institution through discussion with directors, governors and funding bodies, and be used as part of the evidence base for an inspection.

Chapter summary

The main points covered in this chapter are:

- ✓ Assessment measures the achievement of learners, evaluation measures the overall effectiveness of teaching sessions or courses.
- ✓ Evaluation is an ongoing informal process.
- ✓ Formal evaluations can be carried out using either spoken or written techniques.
- ✓ Different discussion techniques can be used to make spoken evaluations more objective and representative.
- ✓ Evaluation questionnaires can use a mixture of open and closed questions.
- ✓ Evaluation should result in an action plan detailing changes to be implemented.
- ✓ Evaluation takes place at all levels, ranging from self-evaluation of teaching sessions to full institutional evaluations of overall provision.

Further reading

Tummons, J. (2011) *Assessing Learning in the Lifelong Learning Sector*. Exeter: Learning Matters.
Although based around the evaluation of assessment processes, Chapter 8 in this book gives a clear and comprehensive coverage of all facets of evaluation, particularly those aspects concerning external bodies.

Hillier, Y. (2011) *Reflective Teaching in Further and Adult Education* (2nd edn). London and New York: Continuum.
Chapter 9 gives detailed coverage of evaluation, evaluation methods and how to deal with the results of evaluation.

Useful websites

Keep up to date with the latest news from Ofsted
http://www.ofsted.gov.uk/
http://www.ofsted.gov.uk/resources/

Learning and Skills Improvement Service
www.lsis.org.uk

15

Microteaching

Chapter overview

When you have worked through this chapter on microteaching you will be able to:

- Plan a microteaching session
- Develop strategies to deliver the teaching
- Justify your choice of methods, resources, assessment and room layout
- Recognise the importance of reflecting on practice in order to improve as a teacher
- Make the most of discussion and feedback after a session
- Develop a plan for your future development

Microteaching explained

It is normally a requirement of any initial teacher education programme that your teaching is observed. This may be an observation of you teaching your own learners, but it is more likely in an introductory course that you will be observed teaching a short extract from a session, and the learners may be your peers. This short extract is variously called peer-group teaching, a 'mini lesson' or 'microteaching'. We will use the term 'microteaching' in this chapter.

Ultimately, as a teacher, you want your learners to be able to use what they have learned in a meaningful way. Similarly, that has been the aim of this book; the microteaching session will allow you to draw together all the knowledge you have gained from this book and test out whether you can put it into practice.

This chapter is intended to help you plan for your microteaching session and give you the maximum opportunity to demonstrate the effectiveness of your teaching skills. The planning techniques that you will need are those you have already covered in previous chapters, but we will now relate these to the more focused microteaching setting.

Planning for microteaching

As part of your course, you are likely to be given guidance on the microteaching task. The guidance is likely to stipulate:

- Length of time for the microteaching
- Where it will be held
- The resources which will be available
- Arrangements/roles for observation and participation
- Planning and documentation requirements
- Guidance on self and peer evaluation.

And may look something like this:

---

1 Devise a learning objective that can be achieved in 30 minutes.
2 Select appropriate learning activity(ies).
3 Bring any learning resources for a class of 12 learners.
4 Bring the plan for the session with you.
5 Be prepared to discuss your teaching with your peer group afterwards.

On the next page you will find a blank plan suitable for a microteaching session. You may choose to use the form we provide and fill in the sections on the plan for your microteaching session as you work through this chapter. The numbers in brackets suggest the order for completion. Your local centre may require you to use a specific format, but this will still address the same or similar features.

Activity 15.1

Fill in the general details about your microteaching – who, where and when – in boxes labelled 1 on the microteaching plan.

You will now want to think about the group you will teach. What will you know in advance about your learners? What kind of learners are they? What do they already know? Later you can use this information to exploit the diversity in the group and plan for differentiation.

Activity 15.2

Fill in box 2 on the microteaching plan.

Microteaching plan

Course: [1]		Group: [1]	
Venue: [1]	Time: [1]	Date: [1]	
Topic/Title: [3]		Aim: [3]	
Learning outcomes: [3]		How each outcome will be assessed: [6]	Checklist of resources required: [5]
Notes on learners: [2]	Differentiation strategies: [7]	Link to Functional Skills: [7]	
Self-evaluation: [9]			

Time [8]	Development [4]	Delivery [4]		Resources [5]	Assessment [6]
		Teacher activity	Learner activity		
	Introduction				
	Middle				
	End				

Achieving Your PTLLS Award, 2nd edition @ Mary Francis and Jim Gould 2013

Next you will be thinking about what new learning you could introduce to this group. If you do not have experience of teaching it is probably best to select a topic that you are already confident about and therefore comfortable with, although you will need to follow whatever local guidelines you are given. If you already have experience then this is a good time to select something new or to try out a specific activity or assessment method. Whichever the case may be, you need to arrive at a topic that will have some relevance and interest for the group you have identified above.

It is advisable to choose a topic which allows the group to be 'themselves' rather than to imagine they are someone else. If you were going to conduct a session on Functional Skills, for instance, you need to find a topic that is suitable for group members rather than asking them to imagine they cannot spell or are limited in their reading skills.

What objective will you set? Hopefully you will remember that a well-written objective will be SMART (if you need to refresh your memory on this refer back to the section on objective writing in Chapter 5). The focus should be on your learners ('At the end of the session *each learner* will be able to......').

For many new teachers the biggest pitfall in selecting learning objectives for microteaching is to be over ambitious for the time allocated. This can result in you, the teacher, getting through your material, but none of your learners doing so! So, think carefully, from the perspective of your learners, about what they will be able to achieve in the available time.

Activity 15.3

Write your topic, aim and learning objectives in the boxes labelled 3 on the microteaching plan.

What kind of objective have you written? Does it involve your learners achieving knowledge, skills or attitudes? What activities will be suitable for this type of objective?

Next, consider how you will develop your content, what 'must' learners know? In Chapter 8 we focused on promoting 'active learning'; now think carefully about how varying activities will be of benefit to learners; a mix of 'you do', 'they do' works well. Remember that you may need to allocate time for switching from one activity to another, particularly if it involves learners moving.

And do not forget that the session needs a beginning, middle and end!

Activity 15.4

Fill in the development and 'delivery' columns, both labelled 4 on the microteaching plan.

What resources will aid learning? In a short session it is best to have few and simple resources. Some form of visual aid or 'the real thing' (see Chapter 9) to highlight the main points in the 'you do' part of the session, and perhaps a handout with instructions or gaps to fill in for the 'they do' part will probably suffice. Remember to exploit whatever you use to its best advantage.

Activity 15.5

Fill in the resources column and resources check box, both labelled 5 on the microteaching plan.

The next stage is to think about how you will assess what your learners have achieved. If you have written a SMART objective at the beginning then you will have a clear idea about how to assess whether or not learners have achieved it. If you are struggling with this, perhaps you need to have another look at your objective. You may be able to include some short quiz or test at the end of the session, but if time is short you may opt for a more informal approach which fits easily with the planned delivery of the session. Chapter 10 will remind you of some possible approaches.

Activity 15.6

Fill in the assessment method(s) in box 6 on the microteaching plan.

The next thing you will want to feel confident about is that you have planned to be inclusive in this microteaching. Are there any individual needs or experiences that you need to be aware of and plan for? In a short session, such as this, it is less likely that you will be able to develop Functional Skills, but are there any particular Functional Skills that will be required in order for learners to achieve the objective?

Activity 15.7

Fill in the sections on differentiation and Functional Skills in box 7 on the microteaching plan.

Managing timing can be more difficult in a microteaching session than it might be in an actual teaching session. Because of the relatively short length of time involved in the microteaching, there is less room for manoeuvre, particularly if you are planning any exercise which is learner-led. The likelihood is that you will run out of time, rather than finish early, so you need to include a few time checks on your plan so that you can pace yourself appropriately.

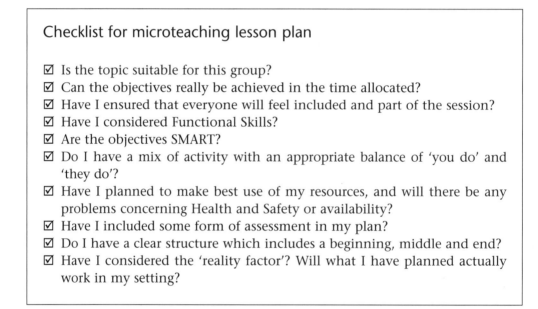

Activity 15.8

Fill in the timing in box 8 on the microteaching plan.

You should now have completed all the sections on your plan, except the box labelled 9, self-evaluation, because that occurs after the session.

There are a lot of small steps here, but following this process will enable you to plan logically for teaching and learning. Now the last step, check your plan against the items below:

Checklist for microteaching lesson plan

☑ Is the topic suitable for this group?
☑ Can the objectives really be achieved in the time allocated?
☑ Have I ensured that everyone will feel included and part of the session?
☑ Have I considered Functional Skills?
☑ Are the objectives SMART?
☑ Do I have a mix of activity with an appropriate balance of 'you do' and 'they do'?
☑ Have I planned to make best use of my resources, and will there be any problems concerning Health and Safety or availability?
☑ Have I included some form of assessment in my plan?
☑ Do I have a clear structure which includes a beginning, middle and end?
☑ Have I considered the 'reality factor'? Will what I have planned actually work in my setting?

Being positive about microteaching

If you have met all the criteria in the checklist above you should now have as near perfect a plan as you can make it. How well you do in microteaching, however, will not just be about planning or teaching knowledge or teaching skills; the attitudes that you bring to the classroom will also influence the outcome.

As we discussed in Chapter 4, it is much easier to relate to learners:

- If you hold them in a positive regard
- If you are relaxed.

If you have not taught before, remember the audience is friendly and wants you to succeed. If you have picked a topic you are comfortable with you should not feel a need to rush or to be afraid of silences.

We are all different and can gain confidence in different ways. So, what might help you achieve a relaxed and positive approach to your teaching?

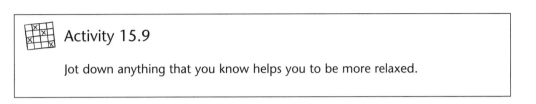

Activity 15.9

Jot down anything that you know helps you to be more relaxed.

Here are some ideas from previous learners / microteachers:

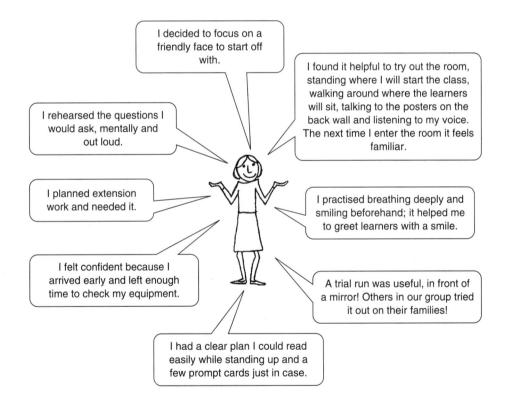

If you plan well and have a positive attitude, this is likely to lead you to a successful microteaching experience.

Delivering the session

In previous chapters you have worked through various aspects that you will now be able to use in delivering your microteaching.

- The beginning will set the tone; when you start aim for eye contact to involve all your learners (for more on this see Chapter 2)
- Communicate the objectives early on and ensure instructions and explanations are clearly communicated (for more on this see Chapter 3)
- Signal clearly to learners when you move from one activity to another, and make sure your session has an obvious beginning, middle and end (for more on this see Chapter 13)
- Treat learners fairly and as individuals. Make sure that you involve them all; use questions where pertinent, listening and responding appropriately. Encourage learners and give praise for contributions (for more on this see Chapters 6, 7 and 8)
- Pace your microteaching to fit the times on your session plan but remember that flexibility is also important (for more on this see Chapter 13)
- Exploit your learning resources (for more on this see Chapter 9)
- Review the session at the end – 'So, what have we learnt?' – and thank learners for their participation (for more on this see Chapter 14).

After the microteaching session

It is vital that you learn from your experience of teaching if you are to develop your skills. You don't necessarily become a better teacher just by doing more and more teaching; experience which is not subjected to thought afterwards may mean repeating mistakes rather than improving. Good teachers become good by learning from their and others' experience, and by engaging in a process of self-evaluation.

We have discussed self-evaluation in the previous chapter. The microteaching experience provides additional opportunities for evaluation through discussion with your tutor and peer group after your session. It is likely that you will also be asked to contribute to discussion about the microteaching sessions of others who are on your course. The purpose of this discussion is to develop your and their teaching rather than finding fault.

So how can you benefit and learn from the microteaching experience? The process of self-evaluation is intended to lead to improved practice. Consider the following sequence:

1 Teach the session.
2 Re-run the session in your mind, asking questions such as:

- What were the significant features?
- What went particularly well? What was I pleased with?
- What did not go as well as I had hoped it would?
- Did anything surprising happen?

3 Analyse the events you identified above and ask, 'Why did that happen?' Engaging in discussion about the 'Why?' forms a very useful part of the post-microteaching discussion.
4 The results of this analysis will lead you to some conclusions about how you might do things differently and, hopefully, more effectively next time.

If you are an observer of microteaching you will also be asking these questions and engaging in reflection.

This cycle of learning is drawn from Kolb (1984), as represented in the diagram below with Kolb's descriptors of each phase in italics.

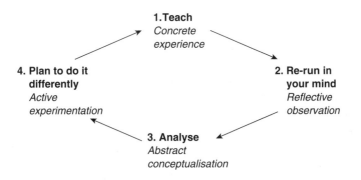

Kolb maintains that we learn through experience, but only if we process that experience and make sense of it.

During the microteaching experience you will learn through observing others and giving feedback to them, as well as being observed yourself and receiving feedback from your tutor or group. It is useful to think about the way in which this feedback is given (see Chapter 8) so that you can provide feedback more effectively to others in your group.

Try to focus on:

- Acknowledging success
- Identifying strengths
- Identifying an area to develop for a future session
- Ideas for improvement.

Ideas for improvement can then be built into an action plan, as we saw in the previous chapter.

Where next?

Once you have successfully completed your introductory teaching course you can continue to develop your teaching through further professional development, particularly if it is well planned.

Professional development involves a process of continual appraisal and updating of the skills, knowledge and understanding relating to the teaching of your subject.

Your development plan should include updating your subject knowledge as well as a focus on developing your teaching. You may well already have ideas about how you can take this forward. Have you considered the following?

☑ Reflect – undertake regular self-evaluation.
☑ Ask your learners.
☑ Watch someone teach.
☑ Arrange to visit an 'expert'.
☑ Go on a course or conference.
☑ Visit another organisation similar to yours.
☑ Search the net for the latest developments in your subject.
☑ Ask someone to observe you.
☑ Keep a learning log or journal.
☑ Continue to read about teaching and learning.
☑ Consider career advice, for example that offered by the University and College Union.
☑ Update your subject specialism through networking with other specialists, professional journals and work experience.

As you near successful completion of your course your thoughts could be turning to the next stage in your professional development as a teacher or trainer. The qualification structure for professionals in the lifelong learning sector is currently under review, but your organisation and the websites below will be able to signpost the next appropriate step for you.

We trust that working through this book will have prepared you for teaching in the lifelong learning sector. It will also have given you a foundation for your future development, an introduction to some educational theory, such as that of Kolb, above, and ideas on how to cite and reference (see Appendix 3) that you will meet again at the next stage. We wish you the best of luck in your future professional life.

→ Reference

Kolb, D. (1984) *Experiential Learning: Experience as the Source of Learning and Development*. Upper Saddle River, NJ: Prentice Hall.

Further reading

Hillier, Y. (2011) *Reflective Teaching in Further Education and Adult Education* (2nd edn). London: Continuum.
Contains useful ideas for continuing professional development.

Roffey-Barentsen, J. and Malthouse, R. (2009) *Reflective Practice in the Lifelong Learning Sector (Achieving QTLS)*. Exeter: Learning Matters Ltd.
In-depth coverage of issues related to reflective practice in the sector.

Useful websites

The University and College Union offers a range of professional resources and free membership to anyone training to teach in the lifelong learning sector
http://www.ucu.org.uk/LSIS
http://www.lsis.org.uk/Pages/default.aspx

Institute for Learning
http://www.ifl.ac.uk/

For more on 14–19
www.education.gov.uk/b00199952/the-education-funding-agency

National Apprenticeship Service
http://www.apprenticeships.org.uk/

For more on Adult Learning and Skills
http://www.bis.gov.uk/Policies/further-education-skills/sfa
http://skillsfundingagency.bis.gov.uk/
http://www.niace.org.uk/

Appendix 1

Mapping the content of the book against current PTLLS requirements

PTLLS Units and Outcomes	Chapter
Roles, Responsibilities and Relationships in Lifelong Learning	
1 Understand own role and responsibilities in identifying and meeting the needs of learners	1
2 Understand the relationships between teachers and other professionals in lifelong learning	1/6
3 Understand own responsibility for maintaining a safe and supportive learning environment	1/2/4
Understanding Inclusive Learning and Teaching in Lifelong Learning	
1 Understand teaching and learning strategies in lifelong learning	8/13
2 Understand how to create inclusive learning and teaching in lifelong learning	6/8/10/11
3 Understand ways to create a motivating learning environment	2/3/4/10
Using Inclusive Learning and Teaching approaches in Lifelong Learning	
1 Plan inclusive learning and teaching sessions	5/12
2 Deliver inclusive learning and teaching sessions	6/8/10
3 Evaluate own practice in delivering inclusive learning and teaching sessions	13/14

Principles of Assessment in Lifelong Learning	
1 Understand types and methods of assessment used in lifelong learning	10/11
2 Understand how to involve learners in the assessment process	10/11
3 Understand requirements for keeping records of assessment in lifelong learning	10/11
Learning and Development alternatives	
Facilitate learning and development in groups	
1 Understand principles and practices of learning and development in groups	7/2/6
2 Facilitate learning and development in groups	7/4
3 Assist groups to apply new knowledge and skills in practical contexts	7
4 Assist learners to reflect on their learning and development undertaken in groups	7/14
Facilitate learning and development with individuals	
1 Understand principles and practice of one-to-one learning and development	7
2 Facilitate one-to-one learning and development	7
3 Assist individual learners in applying knowledge and skills in practical contexts	7/8
4 Assist individual learners to reflect	7/14
Understanding the principles and practice of assessment	
1 Understand the principles and requirements of assessment	10/11
2 Understand different types of assessment method	10/11
3 Understand how to plan assessment	10/11
4 Understand how to involve learners and others in assessment	10/11
5 Understand how to make an assessment decision	10/11
6 Understand quality assurance of the assessment process	10/11
7 Understand how to manage information related to assessment	10/11
8 Understand the legal and good practice requirements in relation to assessment	10/11

Appendix 2   Example session plans

(a) Group plan

Group: AAT Foundation/Certificate	Venue: Room Q3	Time: 17:45–21:15	Date: 23/01/12
Topic/Title: Reports & Returns – VAT		Aims: To introduce the concepts, considerations and calculations for VAT	

Learning Outcomes: Learners will be able to: 1 Define VAT and how it works 2 Recognise the layout of a VAT return form 3 Correctly fill in a VAT return	How each outcome will be assessed: 1 Written exercises 2 Results of groupwork 3 Peer marking exercise	Checklist of resources required: Smart Board tools PowerPoint pres. no. 6 Gapped Handout: 'VAT returns'

Notes on learners: 17 adults (19 years upwards) – wide age range. 30% male – 70% female 11 NVQ – 6 Diploma One Diploma student only started this term One NVQ student transferred from another class only last week There are four students for whom English is not the first language One student is dyslexic One student has mobility problems	Differentiation Strategies: Mix of activity – explanation (aural), PowerPoint & Smart Board (visual), practical exercises (kinaesthetic) As there are a lot of 'little' parts of this topic, I am just putting one 'graduated' exercise of each type within the main body of the text so that the class can all progress through the material at the same rate but at their own level. The longer exercises at the end will be completed by the more able students, giving one-to-one time for those who grasp this less quickly Clarity of speech and straightforward use of English to help ESOL students Explanation of unusual vocabulary Handouts of a suitable font, size and colour for dyslexic student	Links to Functional Skills: Competence in basic Maths and English is expected. Those following the NVQ route are also likely to have been employed in this sector All except the January starter have completed the Bookkeeping to Initial Trial Balance part of the course Literacy – reading and comprehension of official forms Numeracy – simple mathematical operations (addition, subtraction, multiplication, division, calculation of percentages) ICT – volunteers will make contributions on the electronic whiteboard

Self-Evaluation:

Overall, I was quite pleased with the way this session went. The introduction at the start enabled the newer students to feel part of the group; everyone took part and remained involved and responsive throughout the evening. The Smart Board was useful for the presentation and helped to maintain attention. Most of the group came up and used it to make a contribution. This was quite time consuming – took longer than I had anticipated but I feel it was a worthwhile exercise for its positive effects on the dynamic of the group. The graded exercises worked well – most seemed to be working at a level which provided a challenge, and I had some time to spend with those who needed help. I will use this approach again. The peer marking exercise was OK but could have been taken more seriously – became a bit too 'sociable'. Perhaps next time I will mix the pairs up instead of letting them work in the pairs where they always sit.

Time	Development	Delivery		Resources	Assessment
		Teacher Activity	**Learner Activity**		
Intro. 17:45–17:50	Initial admin Arrangements for next few weeks	Explanation	Listen – chance to ask questions	Register	
	Recap of last week's session	Directed questioning	Answers		Q&A
Devel. 17:50–18:05	**What is VAT and how does it work?**	Background, explanation of basic principles	Listen, ask questions	PowerPoint slides 1–4	
18:05–18:15	Input and Output tax	Explanation	Questions Complete Exercise 1	PowerPoint slides 5–9 Gapped Handout	Q&A Exercise results
18:15–18:30	Invoicing	Information and example	Volunteers to fill in gaps on Smart Board	Smart Board	Contributions and questioning
18:30–18:45	Imports and Exports	Explanation	List EU countries Exercise 2 (pairwork)	Gapped Handout	Q&A Monitoring / Observation

(Continued)

18:45–19:00	BREAK				
19:00–19:30	The VAT Return	Describe boxes	Complete example return (small groups)	Smart Board Returns exercise	Group feedback
19:30–20:00	Records, VAT Control, errors and special schemes	Explanation of details		PowerPoint slides 10 & 11 Internet Smart Board	Q&A
20:00–20:45	Practice	Supervision and support as required	Listen, ask questions, make notes as required. Try graduated examples (pairwork)	Gapped Handout	Observation
20:45–20:55	Feedback on answers	Give answers, respond to questions	Peer marking between pairs		Peer marking and questioning
End 20:55–21:00	Conclusion	Summary, next week's topic and reminder of arrangements			

(b) Workshop plan

Course: First Diploma in Media		Module: Video Production	Venue: XX College
	Date: 8 March 2012	Date: 15 March 2012	Date: 22 March 2012
Learner 1	*Outcome/Target:* To complete filming of drama. Film multiple takes and monitor sound through the use of headphones.	*Outcome/Target:* To capture video footage onto Premiere Pro and make rough edit participating as part of a group.	*Outcome/Target:* To complete rough edit and create an audio track using music and sound effects.
	Resource Requirements: Filming kit, DV Tape	*Resource Requirements:* Premiere Pro workstation, DV Tape	*Resource Requirements:* Premiere Pro workstation, CDs, MP3 etc. of Audio Files
	Progress/Evaluation: A wide range of shots filmed and sound monitored effectively. The whole script has now been filmed so editing can begin next lesson.	*Progress/Evaluation:* Contributed well to group work and has assisted in editing at least 2 minutes of video in a logical order. Collect various audio tracks to insert in film by next week.	*Progress/Evaluation:* Audio tracks used to good effect to create a tense atmosphere in the edited film. Next week, insert a title sequence and touch up effects/ transitions to make the edits flow.
Learner 2	*Outcome/Target:* Pre-production work – Treatment and Shooting Schedule must be written, printed off and handed in.	*Outcome/Target:* Begin filming drama with careful reference to shooting schedule and storyboards. Aim to film at least 2 scenes with multiple takes.	*Outcome/Target:* Complete filming of drama by re-shooting conversation scene (with a tripod) and final scene.
	Resource Requirements: PC with Printing facilities. Examples of pre-production forms.	*Resource Requirements:* Pre-production work for reference. Filming kit and DV Tape	*Resource Requirements:* Filming kit, DV Tape
	Progress/Evaluation: Treatment and shooting schedule completed and handed in. Discussed possible improvements which can be made.	*Progress/Evaluation:* Both planned scenes filmed and had time to film additional cut-away shots. Some of the shots are not steady so may need to be re-shot depending on time constraints.	*Progress/Evaluation:* Footage is well filmed with good use of natural lighting and sound. Ready to begin editing next week.

(Continued)

(Continued)

Course: First Diploma in Media	Module: Video Production	Venue: XX College
	Date: 8 March 2012	Date: 15 March 2012	Date: 22 March 2012

	Date: 8 March 2012	Date: 15 March 2012	Date: 22 March 2012
Learner 3	*Outcome/Target:* To use effects and transitions on edited drama to create excitement and tension. *Resource Requirements:* Premiere Pro workstation *Progress/Evaluation:* Worked very well in producing an exciting drama which delivers a strong coherent meaning. Editing skills are of a very high standard.	*Outcome/Target:* To adjust audio levels on edited drama and insert titles. Burn film onto DVD. *Resource Requirements:* Premiere Pro workstation Recordable DVD *Progress/Evaluation:* Drama completed to a near professional standard and put work onto DVD.	*Outcome/Target:* Improve pre-production work following advice from formative assessment feedback. *Resource Requirements:* PC with printing facilities. Previous work with formative feedback sheets. *Progress/Evaluation:* Pre-production work improved following the given advice. Began preparation for oral presentation next lesson.
Learner 4	*Outcome/Target:* Pre-production work – Proposal and Storyboards to be completed, printed off and handed in. *Resource Requirements:* PC with printing facilities. Storyboard sheets & pencils. Examples of pre-production forms. *Progress/Evaluation:* Proposal and storyboards completed and handed in to myself. Both pieces of work although late are of a good quality and do not need to be improved.	*Outcome/Target:* Begin filming drama with careful use of camera work. Aim of filming introduction and main character's action scene. *Resource Requirements:* Pre-production work for reference Filming kit and DV Tape *Progress/Evaluation:* Drama filmed in its entirety to a good standard and ready to begin editing next lesson.	*Outcome/Target:* To capture video footage onto Premiere Pro and make rough edit of a minimum duration of two minutes. *Resource Requirements:* Premiere Pro workstation DV Tape *Progress/Evaluation:* Only one minute's worth of edited material due to problems with the Premiere Pro workstation. Continue with the editing before the next timetabled lesson.

Appendix 3

Citing and referencing

When you write assignments, you will be drawing on:

- The content of sessions on your teacher education course
- Your own experience and ideas
- The ideas expressed by others in books and other sources.

We are providing this Appendix to help you with the last of these three.

All assignments written at this level use other people's thoughts and ideas. It is usual to build upon existing knowledge rather than reinvent the wheel each time you tackle an assignment. You are therefore expected to use other people's work to introduce new ideas or support your own arguments. Quotes are normally used when they:

- Sum something up in a novel but concise manner: ... *'statistics can be used in much the same way as a drunk uses a lamp-post: for support rather than illumination'*.
- Define a particular bit of terminology: ... a support role is *'one which directly supports teaching and learning but for which teaching is not the main purpose'*.
- Directly support a point you want to make: ... also suggests that *'it is not easy to estimate how long an activity will take'*.

When you use a quote, you are expected to acknowledge this, identifying which parts of your assignment have been taken from someone else's book or article. When you do this you are **citing**.

When your tutor reads your assignment they may find your quote interesting and want to read more. You therefore have to give them sufficient information to allow them to track down the original piece of work from which you have quoted. This is **referencing**.

Let us take an example.

You have to complete an assignment on negotiating ground rules for next week and have just found an appropriate quote to use which is:

> *Once the rules are established you may be able to bend them a bit, but be fair and consistent even here.*

You found it on page 104 of a book called *Teaching Today*. This is the fourth edition of this book which Geoff Petty wrote in 2009 and is published by Nelson Thornes. You want to include this in your assignment on ground rules. How do you go about citing and referencing?

To cite

You have to give the reader a signal that this is someone else's work. There are two ways in which we can do this:

1   Run the quote into the text, but surround it with ' ':

    ... text text text 'Once the rules are established you may be able to bend them a bit, but be fair and consistent even here' text text text text text ...

    This is the procedure for shorter quotes (less than 30 words).

2   If you decide to use a longer quote, it tends to get lost in the text, so for longer quotes, separate the quote out from the main body of text by leaving a blank line before and after and indenting the quote.

    ... text text text:

    > Once the rules are established you may be able to bend them a bit, but be fair and consistent even here. As far as possible, there should be a similar approach to rules and regimes from all the teachers whom the students experience.

    text text text text text ......

    This is the procedure for longer quotes (approx. 30 words or more).

Having signalled the quote we now have to indicate whose work it is. To include all of the information above at this stage disrupts the flow of the reader, so initially we only need to supply sufficient information to contextualise the quote. You therefore give the name of the author and the year of publication of the source book. If the quote is a 'direct lift' from the book, then you also need to supply the number of the page upon which the quote can be found. If you do not, the reader will have to scan through the whole book to find it. Fine if it is on page 1 but a bit frustrating if it is on page 659! If it is a theory or idea that is mentioned, the page number can be omitted as the reader will be able to track it down by using the Index of the book.

So, using the above example, citing would look like this:

1   ... text text, although Petty (2009: 104) says 'Once the rules are established you may be able to bend them a bit, but be fair and consistent even here' text text text text text ...

2   ... text text, as Petty (2009: 104) points out:

Once the rules are established you may be able to bend them a bit, but be fair and consistent even here. As far as possible, there should be a similar approach to rules and regimes from all the teachers whom the students experience.

text text text text text ......

Or

... text text text:

Once the rules are established you may be able to bend them a bit, but be fair and consistent even here. As far as possible, there should be a similar approach to rules and regimes from all the teachers whom the students experience. (Petty, 2009: 104)

text text text text text ......

So much for citing.

To reference

We are now looking to tell the reader how they can track down the quote. We have told them the author, the year of publication and the page number (if required). We now have to tell them the title and edition of the book and the publisher. You display this information at the end of the assignment under the title of 'Reference List' in the following sequence:

1   Author
2   Year (this links the author to the particular book we are using. It is possible that we may have quoted from more than one book from the same author. The year of publication links the quote to the specific book)
3   Title of Book (normally underlined, bold or italicised to make it stand out)
4   Edition of Book (if not first edition)
5   Publisher and their location

In our example the entry on the Reference List would be as follows:

Petty, G. (2009) *Teaching Today* (4th edn). Cheltenham: Nelson Thornes.

If you use a number of different sources, you would list these in your reference list in alphabetical order of author's name. There are further refinements to the system but this should get you started and, hopefully, feeling more confident about the process.

You may wish to reference material you have found on the Internet. If so, care should be taken to make sure that whatever you wish to quote comes from a credible source. Who is the author, what qualifications do they have, are they really an authority on this subject? Having satisfied yourself that your source is legitimate, you proceed in much the same way as with a book, citing the author (or perhaps organisation) and either the year of the article or the year in which it was placed on the web. The reference should include the title of the article, the website address (URL) and the date you accessed the information. Web pages are often changed or modified which is why the date of access is required.

You will find the following websites useful in helping you to format your references.

http://www.neilstoolbox.com/bibliography-creator/
http://www.lc.unsw.edu.au/onlib/ref_elec1.html

The following text covers every eventuality for referencing purposes and gives useful examples in all cases:
Pears, R. and Shields, G. (2010) *Cite Them Right: The Essential Referencing Guide.* (8th edn). Basingstoke: Palgrave Macmillan.

Glossary of terms

Active learning   Techniques that encourage learning through 'doing' and interacting with the material being learned.

Aim   A general statement outlining what the teacher hopes to achieve during the session or programme of learning.

Assertive   Expressing yourself in a self-confident manner.

Assessment   The process of measuring the achievement of learners; judgement is made as to whether learning objectives have been met or not.

Assessment records   The documents used to record the outcome of an assessment; these could be:

- An organisational pro forma or log such as a candidate record sheet
- A document provided by an outside agency such as an Awarding Body
- A personal log held by the tutor or learner.

Authentic   In an assessment, the need to be certain that it is the learner's own work that is being assessed.

Awarding Body   An organisation that issues course documentation and certificates nationally accredited courses.

Blended learning   A combination of different approaches to learning, usually including some form of e-learning, used to deliver a specific programme or part of a programme.

Communication   The transfer of information, from one person to another, with the intention of bringing about a response.

Competence   The acquisition of knowledge, skills and abilities to a level of expertise sufficient to be able to perform a job role in an appropriate work setting to national standards.

Competence-based assessment   When a candidate is judged against a specific set of skills and attributes required in an occupational setting.

Current   Evidence that shows that the candidate can perform competently at the time of the assessment.

Diagnostic assessment   The assessment used to discover the relative strengths and weaknesses in a learner's work and determine future action.

Differentiation   The strategies used by teachers to manage the learning environment in such a way that they cater for the full range of individual difference.

Direct Evidence   Evidence produced by the candidate.

Diversity   The recognition of the uniqueness of each learner in a typical learning group.

e-assessment   The end-to-end electronic assessment processes where ICT is used for the presentation for assessment activity, and the recording of responses.

e-learning   Learning that is delivered, enabled or mediated using electronic technology.

Embed   To incorporate something (Functional Skills) into a greater whole (subject specialism) so it becomes an integral part.

e-portfolio   A collection of evidence presented in electronic format.

Equitable   In assessment, a method of assessment which does not disadvantage anyone who takes it.

Equality   To be subjected to fair treatment – the same as others, equivalence. Possessing the same rights and value equal to all others in a specific group.

Evaluation   Gathering information to give a measure of the effectiveness of the session or programme that has been delivered. The teacher can then use this information to improve future sessions or programmes.

Extrinsic   Acting upon the person but originating from the external environment.

Feedback   The giving of information to a learner or teacher on their performance, allowing them to identify particular strengths to build upon or weaknesses to be improved upon.

Formative assessment   An assessment is formative when it is undertaken to measure progress. Formative assessment results are used to inform future learning and give feedback on progress made.

Functional Skills   The core elements of English, Maths and ICT that provide an individual with the essential knowledge, skills and understanding that will enable them to operate confidently, effectively and independently in life and at work.

Ground rules   An agreed code of behaviour within a learning group.

Icebreaker   An activity, normally used at the beginning of a session or programme of teaching, which encourages learners to communicate with each other. It is designed to break down the barriers that invariably exist when a group of people meet for the first time.

Inclusion   The process of making learners feel that they are fully part of the learning and social environment.

Indirect Evidence   Evidence used when competence cannot be directly observed; used to infer competence.

Induction   Programme to introduce learners to their new environment and its procedures.

Initial assessment   The process of identifying appropriate learning programmes for individual learners based on level, suitability and the possible need for additional learning support.

Intrinsic   Stemming from inside the individual rather than from any external source.

Learning objectives   A statement of what is to be learned; objectives are written in a manner that is specific, expressing learning in an active form that can be relatively easily measured and assessed.

Learning styles   The particular way in which an individual prefers to learn; the preferred way in which learners take in and process the information received during teaching.

Microteaching   A scaled down teaching performance delivered to a small group of peers during a short time period and accompanied by reasonably detailed feedback.

Motivation   The force or reason behind a particular action.

Non-verbal communication   Any communication that does not involve the spoken word; this includes body language, facial expressions and noises.

Ofsted   The organisation responsible for inspecting care for young people and education and training for learners of all ages.

Personal action plan   A systematic method of identifying and recording the strategies to be employed by an individual learner, in achieving a given goal or goals within a specified time frame.

Personalisation   The process of tailoring delivery of a programme to the individual needs or characteristics of the participating learners.

Quality assurance   The process by which standards are checked and monitored on a regular basis.

Reliability   The consistency of measurement achieved in the use of an assessment method. The results of assessment can be considered reliable if the same candidate would achieve the same result for the assessment if it were taken on another occasion or with another teacher.

Role   The functions assigned to and behaviours expected of an individual who is acting in a particular capacity.

Self-concept   The mental image or perception that an individual has of themselves.

Skills analysis   The breaking down of a skill into its component parts or sub-skills.

Stereotype   A conventional, formulaic and oversimplified conception, opinion, or image of a specific group.

Summative assessment   An assessment made to determine the final level of achievement; this is not necessarily at the end of a complete learning programme, but could be at the end of a particular stage in it (for example, the end of a learning module on a specific subject which will not be assessed again).

Transparent   In a given form of assessment, it is clear what is being assessed and how judgements are being made.

Validity   The extent to which an assessment method measures what it is supposed to measure.

Verifier   A person who checks the assessment practices of teachers to ensure consistency and maintain standards; an internal verifier (IV) normally works within one organisation; an external verifier (EV) works for an Awarding Body and verifies assessment practices normally across several centres.

Vocational   Relating to training which is intended to prepare learners for an occupation.

Index

Action plans 192–3
Active listening 28
Aim 53–55
Assertive discipline 39, 121
Assessment 128–154
  Checklist 141
  Competence-based *see* Competence-
    based assessment
  Diagnostic 139
  E-assessment 131
  Evidence 151–2
  Formal 133
  Formative 139
  Informal 133
  Initial 64–65
  Methods 129
  Peer 140
  Purposes 132
  Preparing learners 141
  Records of 144, 153
  Self 140
  Summative 139
Attention 91–2
  Span 66, 91–92
Attitudes 102–104
  Structure of 103–104
  Teaching of 102–109

Basic skills *see* Functional Skills
Behaviour
  Aggressive 44–45
  Assertive 45–46
  Management 38–46
  Passive 45
Bias 138
Blended Learning 124
Bloom, B. 69
Boundaries 9
Buzz groups 78, 90, 187

Citing 216–217
Classroom management
  42–46
see also behaviour management

Code of practice 7
Communication 13–15, 22, 24–33
One and two way 14–15
  Barriers to 31–33
  Non–verbal 29–30
  Voice 25–27
Competence 147
Competence-based assessment 147–153
  Checklist 153
  In the workplace 150
  Roles 149
  Sources of evidence 151
  Stages 149–153

Dale, E. 90
Demonstration 98–100
Differentiation 68
  Strategies 69–71
Disability 8, 72
Discipline *see* behaviour management
Discussion 104–106
  Checklist 106
Diversity 67

E-assessment 131–132
E-portfolio 152
E-resources 120–125
Environment 12–23, 35–36
  Learning 13–23, 36
  Physical 13–15, 36
  Social 13, 15–21, 36
Equality 71–72
Essay 131
Evaluation 183–194
  Methods 185–189
  Questionnaires 189
see also self-evaluation
Every Child Matters (ECM) 7

Feedback
  Constructive 143–144
  Giving 101–102, 144, 152
First impressions 15–17
Flip chart 117

Functional Skills 155–167
  Embedding 159
  Mapping 159

Ground rules 15, 18

Handouts 117–119
Health and Safety 8

Ice-breakers 20–21, 125
ICT *see* Functional Skills
Inclusion 68
Individual
  Action plan 192–193
  Differences 65–67
  Learning plan 85
Induction 16–17
Initial assessment *see*
  assessment
Institutional support 72
  Internal and external 10
Introductions 20

Kolb, D. 205

Learning
  Activities/methods 59–60,
    88–109
  Active and passive 90
  Contract 86
  Objectives 53, 55–58
  Styles 65
Lecture 89
Legislation 7–8
Lifelong learning sector 1–3
Literacy *see* Functional Skills

Maslow, A.H. 36–37
Methods *see* learning activities
Models 113–114
Microteaching 196–206
Motivation 34–37
  Intrinsic 35–37
  Extrinsic 35–37
Multiple choice questions 130

Needs, hierarchy of *see* Maslow
Non-verbal communication 29
  see also communication
Note taking 92
Numeracy *see* Functional Skills

Objectives *see* learning objectives
Observation 131
Openings 17–18
Overhead projector 119

Planning 48–60, 167– 181
  Cycle 53
  Decisions 169
  Examples 170–172, 179, 210–214
  For groups 170–178
  For microteaching 197–202
  For workshop/project 178–181
  Formats 170–171, 179–181, 198–199, 218
  Purposes 167
  Structure 172
  see also session plans
Post-16 education *see* lifelong learning
PowerPoint 120–121
Professional Development 206
PTLLS 1, 3, 208–209

Qualified Teacher Status (QTLS) 163
Quality
  Assurance 153
  Improvement 194
Question and answer 93–96

Reality factor 59
Record keeping 144–145
Referencing 216–218
Reflection 205
Reliability 137–138
Resources 111–127
  Checklist 126
  Design 115
  Evaluation of 125
  Range of 112–125
Responsibilities *see* role
Role 3–7
Role play 106–109
Room layout 14–15
Round 82, 187

Self-actualisation 38, 39
Self-concept 40–41
Self disclosure 74
Self-evaluation 177–178, 204–206
Session plans 172–181
see also planning
  Checklist 178
Skill 96

Skills
   Analysis 97–98
   Practice 100–101
   Teaching of skills based subjects 96–102
Skills for Life 156
see also Functional Skills
SMART 58, 64, 134–135, 172
Snowball 20, 78, 187
Summarising 28–29

Teaching and learning approaches
see learning activities/methods

Theory, teaching of 89–96
Timing 173–174

VAK 66
Validity 136
Virtual learning environment 124
Vocational qualifications 148

Watkins, C. 45
Whiteboard 116–117
   Interactive whiteboard 122

978-1-84860-616-6   978-1-84920-030-1   978-1-84920-114-8

978-1-84860-713-2   978-1-84920-076-9   978-1-84920-126-1   978-1-84920-078-3

Find out more about these titles and our wide range
of books for education students and practitioners at
www.sagepub.co.uk/education

EXCITING EDUCATION TEXTS FROM SAGE